Travel
with Others
Without Wishing They'd Stayed Home

Nadine Nardi Davidson

PRINCE PUBLISHING
LOS ANGELES

Library of Congress Cataloging-in-Publication Data
Davidson, Nadine Nardi
    Travel with others: without wishing they'd stayed home /
Nadine Nardi Davidson. — 1st ed.
        p. cm.
    Includes index.
    Preassigned LCCN: 98-65256
    ISBN: 0-9658194-3-4
    1. Travel etiquette. 2. Travel. I. Title.
BJ2137.D38 1998   395'.5
                                        QBI98-208

For my parents:
William and Anne Nardi

Acknowledgments

I wish to thank my husband, Dr. Harold Davidson, for many wonderful travel experiences; Dr. Claire Panosian, Dr. Arlene Westley, Dr. Julie Ryan and Sandra Hatch for their expert advice; Joan Prestine, Celeste Mannis, Beverly Baroff, Estellaleigh Franenberg, Ann Schuessler, David Marchese and Lloyd Robinson for their helpful suggestions. I am deeply grateful to all those travelers who shared their experiences and made this book possible. I also wish to thank the following professionals for their contributions to this work: Marilyn Ross, printing; Sharon Goldinger, editing; Joyce Ananian, indexing; Joel Friedlander, book design and typography; Ken Merfeld, cover photo; George Foster, cover design.

Warning - Disclaimer

TABLE OF CONTENTS

Preface

The rain kicked the windshield like a spoiled child in a bad temper. From the backseat I strained to see the double yellow line on the turnpike that connected Oklahoma City and Tulsa.

It was 11 P.M. and my mother was aggravated. "Why don't you ever listen to me? There were plenty of vacancies back there, but no, you had to drive on to one more town."

Behind the wheel, my father was silent. Like scratching a mosquito bite, his silence only made her voice swell.

Her monologue of I-told-you-sos continued for two more miles. Finally, Dad erupted without warning in a torrent of curses and a predictable "Get off my back."

I perched uncomfortably on the edge of the seat and tried to change the subject. I was seven years old but vowed then that when I grew up and got married, I would never complain. After all, what was the big deal? We always found a motel eventually. It wasn't the end of the world.

It was 11 P.M. and it was raining buckets. This time it was thirty years later on the Connecticut turnpike that linked New York with New Haven. My husband was still complaining as he had every hour on the hour since our flight took off from Los Angeles to Kennedy Airport.

"I hate staring at the wall on an airplane. You're a travel agent. You know I hate bulkhead seats."

"The other seats were full. What did you expect me to do— have the airline bump everyone else out of their seats to make room for you?"

"You're my travel agent. I expect you to do whatever it takes to get row three!"

"What's the difference? The seats in row one are exactly the same size and color as the seats in row three. Besides, if you hadn't changed the reservation so you could spend a few more hours in the office, we would have had row three."

He was angry with me and I was mad at him for being angry with me. Why did we have to go through these unpleasantries each time we took what was supposed to be a relaxing trip? How could we avoid them?

One of the first steps in eliminating these tense moments is the recognition that there are different types of travelers, with different needs and different expectations. This book will help you identify these needs and expectations so that, no matter whom you travel with, you'll be able to minimize anxieties and maximize the enjoyment of each travel experience.

Identifying Traveler Type

What type of traveler are you and those you travel with? Understanding your differences is one key to successful trip planning.

In my twenty-plus years as a travel consultant, I've worked with travelers from ages 9 to 90 with budgets ranging from $5 a day to "money is no object." They vary from businessmen who must fly to Chicago in February (no matter that the wind-chill factor is –57 degrees), to honeymooners with high romantic expectations, to "empty nesters" ready for that once-in-a-lifetime vacation.

The following general categories cover the most common types of travelers. Which best describes you? See if you can find yourself.

The Travel Enthusiast

There is one group for whom travel is a habitual and necessary "fix." "Travel enthusiasts" may be school teachers, accountants, students or housewives, but they *live* for the next trip, the next adventure, the next experience. Their excitement about their latest adventure shines at parties and the office. They may have lost baggage, taken the wrong train and roomed with cockroaches, but no matter.

It was all part of *experiencing* the place. All inconvenience dims in the brightness of their enthusiasm. Some of these people even become travel agents. Most, however, seem to share a common background. They began traveling while still students, usually in college. Often, their first experience was a year of study abroad, sometimes with fellow classmates, but often alone.

Why did these first adventures produce lifetime travelphiles? For most of us who first traveled as students, it wasn't just the camaraderie with fellow students or the first taste of freedom from the supervision of parents that we experienced, but something more profound. Making decisions and quick judgments about the people we met along the way became an exercise in self-discovery. We were on our own and we could handle it. The struggle to make ourselves understood in high-school French and self-taught German required an outgoing spirit. It pulled us outside of ourselves and it was a glorious high.

The important thing to remember about the enthusiast is that travel is an essential part of living. Like Italians need pasta, the enthusiast needs regular doses of travel to feel alive and well.

The Adventurer

"Adventurers" exhibit all the symptoms of enthusiasts with one added ingredient. The presence of some physical challenge or physical risk is part of the thrill they seek. It is not enough for them to *see* the Himalayas. They must trek through the mountains on foot in a test of their endurance of altitude and cold. Their ski vacations start with a helicopter drop on an uncharted course so they can float through virgin powder up to their waists. While they are kayaking down the Colorado River or bicycling through Europe, the sights and sounds are only the appetizers. The main course is the physical challenge. The important thing to remember about adventurers is that you can kill yourself trying to keep up with them.

The Sportsman

"Sportsmen," or "sportswomen" for that matter, may have no interest in travel but love to spend their vacations on their sport, be it fishing, golf, tennis, wind surfing or skiing. The surest way to motivate sportsmen to travel is with a promise of the ultimate 18 holes, the biggest blue marlin or a resort with unlimited court time. Sportsmen don't have to be participants. Some avid sports spectators are the first to make reservations for Wimbledon, the Super Bowl or the Kentucky Derby.

The Relaxer

Nine times out of ten, "relaxers" want to spend their vacations on a beach anywhere there is absolutely, positively nothing to do. Frequently, relaxers are businesspersons who work long hours and never get enough sleep, or mothers who just want enough time away from the kids to soak in a tub or let their nail polish dry completely. The bodies of relaxers cry out for renewal. Their ideal vacation spot may not have a beach, but it will be a resort where they don't have to lift a finger, and preferably, not even their heads.

The Beach Bum

"Beach bums" differ from relaxers because they *must* have a beach and guaranteed sunshine to bring home enviable tans. Their goal may include relaxation, but chances are beach bums are also into water sports like surfing, snorkeling, scuba diving or water skiing.

The Comfort Seeker

"Comfort seekers" wouldn't think of budging from their own abodes, unless assured a deluxe hotel in a meticulously kept setting (no view of poverty or substandard housing, please) and wonderful cuisine served with the most attentive service. Spoiled? Not necessarily. For comfort seekers, the thrill is not *where* they go but *how* they go. Sometimes comfort-seekers are the rich and famous who just want what they are used to—the best. And sometimes they are average-income individuals whose thrill in travel is to experience the luxury they can't afford on a day-to-day basis.

The Culturist

"Culturists" travel to immerse themselves in another culture and learn about the people, their customs or their language. These travelers generally prefer to vacation in one city or country for a couple of weeks or more to get a *feel* for life there. They enjoy meeting people and making new friends, shopping in local markets and sightseeing. Culturists, if not history lovers, have at least a reverence for historical sights. They like to browse in art museums, see the local folk dances and music festivals and generally soak up all the culture a place has to offer.

The Shopper

Most travelers, regardless of type, will spend some time snapping up bargains that can't be found at home or methodically searching out souvenirs for family and friends. "Shoppers," by contrast, travel to shop. Anything else they do on vacation is relegated to hours when the shops are closed.

The Discoverer

"Discoverers" seek out destinations that are firsts, if not in the *Guinness Book of World Records,* at least among family and friends. Discoverers will be the first to plunk down a deposit for a commercial flight to outer space. Discoverers visited China before it opened to tourists and Papua New Guinea when there was still an errant headhunter or two. The important thing to remember if you're a discoverer type is that few people may share this thrill of the unknown, and you may have to search the world or the National Geographic Society for someone to travel with.

WHAT KIND OF TRAVELER ARE YOU?

Most travelers are combinations of one or more types. To discover your dominant type, read the questions that follow and circle the answer that *best* fits you, whether or not you've been to the destination referred to.

1. I would rather travel to
    A. A tropical paradise with a great beach.
    B. An exciting city in Europe.
    C. An exotic place in an undeveloped country.
    D. Any place I can participate in my favorite sport (golf, tennis, diving, skiing, boating, riding, swimming, etc.).

2. I would be most excited if I were invited on a trip to
    A. See the gorillas in Africa in their natural habitat.
    B. Go whitewater rafting on a river with class IV rapids.
    C. Stay at a deluxe resort in Bali, Indonesia.
    D. Go shopping in Paris.

3. Given a choice of the four trips below, I would most likely
    A. Camp out with the primitive tribes of the Amazon.
    B. Visit Quebec and Nova Scotia in Canada.

    C. Take a walking trek up and down the Himalayas.

    D. Relax in Maui, Hawaii.

4. If I had a leisure day while on a business trip to Los Angeles, I would most likely

    A. Participate in a specific sport such as golf, tennis, biking, sailing, fishing, scuba diving, etc.

    B. Go sightseeing.

    C. Go shopping.

    D. Go to the beach.

5. When friends or relatives tell me about their trips, the first question I am likely to ask them is

    A. What hotels and restaurants did you like the best?

    B. What did you see and do there?

    C. What things did you buy there?

    D. How's the beach there?

6. If I had a day free while in Kenya, I would

    A. Go hot-air ballooning.

    B. Stay at a beach on the Indian Ocean.

    C. Visit a Masai village.

    D. Stay at the hotel and play my favorite sport.

    E. Go into town and shop.

7. If I had one week to see the Greek islands, I would

    A. See several islands on a deluxe cruise.

    B. Rent a private villa on one island for the whole week.

    C. Fly to three islands and see what I could in two or three days on each island.

    D. Stay with a local family on one island.

8. If I won a one-week trip to one of the following for New Year's, I would choose

    A. A week of opera, concerts and a New Year's Eve ball in Vienna, Austria.

    B. A week of a combination dog sled and reindeer ride to the land of the midnight sun in Finland.

    C. A week's tour of the best shopping spots in Paris.

    D. A week at a Club Med (all-inclusive sports-oriented resort) in the Caribbean.

9. If I won one of the following guided tours, I would choose

    A. A trip to the major sights on mainland China including stays at first-class hotels.

    B. A bicycle trip around Colorado in the summer.

    C. A tour of France's gourmet restaurants and luxury country hotels.

    D. A stay at a first-class beach hotel in Hilton Head, South Carolina.

10. What really makes a trip memorable is

    A. The local people I meet and friends I make there.

    B. The wonderful hotels or inns where I stay.

    C. The bargains I buy.

    D. The sights I see.

    E. The sport (golf, tennis, etc.) I play there.

DIRECTIONS FOR SCORING

1. Look at the answer you chose for question 1 above and circle the corresponding letter(s) in row 1 of the chart below. For example, if your answer to question 1 is *B*, circle all the *B*s in the first row.

2. Do the same for questions 2 to 10.

3. Count the number of circled letters in the first column (Travel Enthusiast) and write the total at the bottom of the chart.

4. Do the same for the remaining columns.

Scoring Chart

	Travel Enthusiast	Adventurer	Sportsman	Relaxer	Beach Bum	Comfort Seeker	Culturist	Shopper	Discoverer
1.	C	A	D	C	B	B	C	B	A
2.	B	C	B	A	A	D	C	C	C
3.	C	D	D	A	B	B	B	D	D
4.	A	D	A	B	B	C	B	A	D
5.	B	D	B	B	B	C	B	A	A
6.	A	B	A	D	C	C	C	E	B
7.	C	B	B	C	C	A	D	A	B
8.	B	D	D	B	B	C	A	A	D
9.	B	D	D	A	A	A	A	C	D
10.	D	D	E	D	D	C	A	B	B
Totals:									

The column or columns with the highest scores should reveal your traveler type. Since many travelers are combinations of travel types, you may have the same score in two or more columns. A travel enthusiast, for example, could also be a culturist and a sportsman also an adventurer.

Now that you know what type you are, try identifying your travel companions, past and future. What kind of travelers are they? If uncertain, give them the test.

ONE

How to Survive Traveling with Your Spouse

Advantages

An advantage of traveling with your spouse is the feeling of security that comes from being two rather than one. Two walking together are less likely than one to be a mugger's target. When a pack of street kids jostles away your wallet in Rome, hopefully your spouse's wallet will still be intact and healthy enough to get you home. Then too, if you get sick along the way, you can send your spouse with a Berlitz book to play charades at a local pharmacy. You'll always have an escort for evening entertainment and at least one dance partner (assuming dancing continued after marriage). Most importantly, you'll have someone to share the experience and the memories—and someone to correct you when you narrate the trip *your* way.

Disadvantages

Your freedom to go where you want and to travel as you please is limited by consideration for your spouse's preferences or objections. Since two is a comfortable number for dinner or a disco, you'll be less likely to seek company and, hence, less likely to meet other people. But most important, a trip with your spouse can be a trying experience if you are not the same type of traveler.

According to Dr. Arlene Westley, an Irvine, California–based marriage and family therapist, "Couples and families frequently come into therapy after a vacation together. Between jobs, errands and television, people often find ways to avoid their partners. An average couple spends less than thirty minutes a week talking to each other. When these couples find themselves together 24 hours a day on vacation, the result can be very stress producing."

Fortunately, there are ways to ensure that you will enjoy your time together.

Making the Transition from One to Two

Even if you and your spouse are as different as Attila the Hun and Marie Antoinette, traveling can be a positive experience if you adjust for the differences. The first step is to define what you both like and dislike in a vacation.

Recently, the excited wife of a business client called me at the travel agency. She and her husband wanted to plan a vacation. "Anywhere in particular?" I asked. "London and Paris and Rome," she answered. "And Switzerland—I hear it's beautiful. And I want to see that mad king's castle—in Germany. And we want to shop in Florence, and I thought we could end up in Venice." I told her I would put together a suggested itinerary we could go over when she and her husband came in.

A few days later, her husband, John, called to change the time of their appointment. "Fine," I told him. "The suggested itinerary for Europe is ready."

"Europe!" he gagged. "I don't want to schlep all over Europe. I'm dead tired. I just want to collapse on a beach somewhere."

"Well, Trudy mentioned Europe an—"

"No way," he interrupted. "She's—"

"Why don't we discuss it when you're both here," I suggested.

When they came in, we faced the question of where they would spend their vacation. The tension was as thick as the pigeon droppings in San Marco Square in Venice. John was angry and Trudy was disappointed. And the trip hadn't even started.

There was obviously a lack of communication about their individual expectations for this vacation. John was a relaxer whose idea of a great vacation was to do nothing. As a regional manager for a computer software company, he spent an average of 10 hours a week in an airplane, sometimes visiting two cities in one day. Trudy was a homemaker. Taking care of three children was time consuming but not particularly exciting. She was ready for a change of scenery and culture. This was her chance to see the places she'd read and dreamed about. "I'll go crazy after two days of doing nothing," she protested. "I'm stuck at home all year. This is my only chance to get out and see something."

We finally settled on a trip that would accommodate both of them. They would go first to a beach hotel on the French Riviera where John could rest. If Trudy got bored, she could shop in Monte Carlo or tour the royal palace. They would then fly to Paris for a week of leisurely sightseeing prior to returning home a few days before John's vacation ended, time enough to recuperate from jet lag before going back to work.

While this compromise meant neither John nor Trudy would have an "ideal" vacation, neither felt cheated.

Trade-Off Negotiations

Some husbands and wives are already experienced in trade-off negotiations: "I'll play golf with you at St. Andrew's in Scotland if we can go to the ballet in London." If carried too far, this method of compromise has its pitfalls. Negotiation can become complicated and a battle for one-upmanship. If you play golf two days, is that equivalent to two ballets or one ballet and one museum? Negotiating for every objective can be time consuming too, and for every agreement, there is one who sacrifices, albeit willingly.

You Don't Always Have to Compromise

In travel, as in marriage, sometimes you have to give up something to get something else in return. But sometimes it's better if you don't compromise.

The first time I traveled with my husband, Harold, to Paris, I coaxed him to the Louvre as a "must see." I had already been to Paris and didn't want him to miss something that had given me so much pleasure. He protested mildly and once we were inside his impatience began to mount.

"It's a museum. Why did we come here?"

"It's one of the greatest museums in the world. Even the *Mona Lisa* is here. You know, Leonardo da Vinci's *Mona Lisa*. Maybe you've heard of it." (I could be sarcastic too.)

Three minutes later we stood on tiptoe straining our necks to glimpse the painting over the heads of a tour group. Harold looked at his watch, "Okay, we've seen it. Let's go." How could anyone be so indifferent to world-class art? I was furious that he refused to enjoy the museum as much as I did. We stomped out of the Louvre in silence.

On subsequent trips to Europe, he would give up time to accompany me to churches or museums in spite of his feeling that "Once you've seen one, you've seen them all." I always felt rushed by his inevitable glances at his watch, never having time to savor each work of art separately. We finally realized that our compulsion to see and do everything together was not a law carved in stone and only resulted in two dissatisfied people.

Now when we travel, I sometimes trek to museums alone while my husband utilizes the time to call his office and work on the business he's brought along, and neither one of us feels that we're missing something.

If you and your spouse don't share the same interests, the key is to plan time for those activities you each want to do on your own. Then you can share your enthusiasm for the acoustics in St. Paul's Cathedral and still get a firsthand description of the cricket match you missed. But resist the impulse to say "Boy, did you miss something!" That psychology is apt to provoke a response like "No, you're the one who missed something." Spread enthusiasm, not superiority.

Who Cares about the Hotel Room?

A client asked me to book her and her husband into Europe's famous hostelries. This was their first trip out of the country, but Linda had been planning it for years—clipping enticing articles and photographs from magazines on places like England's Thornbury Castle and Burgenstock's Park Hotel and scratching notes whenever a friend insisted, "Darling, you absolutely must stay at the Palace in St. Moritz. You'll adore it."

Married while her husband was still in graduate school, only now, five years later, did they have the time and the funds for a honeymoon. Above all, Linda wanted a romantic experience. She pictured herself sipping wine with her husband on the terrace of Villa D'Este on Lake Como in northern Italy. In France's Loire Valley, they would sleep in a twelfth-century chateau whose bedroom walls once blushed at the escapades of more princely occupants.

Her husband, Bob, blushed too when I told him the rates for

this rendezvous with history. Although an avid sightseer, he had no use for such trimmings. "Who cares about the hotel room? We're only going to sleep there. Besides, we can't afford those places."

To Bob, walking hand in hand along the Seine River would be romantic. Tossing a coin in the Fountain of Trevi or stealing a kiss behind one of the few remaining pillars of the Parthenon would be romantic. And *free*.

Budget considerations are a common source of conflict for couples planning a vacation. Linda felt that Bob could divert some of the funds he would "throw away" on his video collection for the trip. It was a matter of priorities. We compromised and put them in first-class and superior tourist-class hotels most of the time with a "big splurge" hotel thrown in here and there.

Solutions are tougher, however, when the disparity between your budget and your expectations is as wide as the registration line at a convention of sumo wrestlers. To create an affordable vacation, one husband mapped out a train trek across Europe with overnights at bed and breakfast inns or economy hotels. His wife, a comfort seeker, refused to go.

"Why should I give up my king-size bed and Jacuzzi bathtub to be uncomfortable for two weeks? I'd rather stay home." She did. Her husband went alone while she waited for their next vacation which, they decided, would be at a resort close to home. Without the cost of international airfares, they could afford a domestic deluxe hotel for a few days.

Sometimes it's not the budget as much as the destination that's objectionable. When a colleague, Eva, went to Kenya with a group of travel agents, her husband, Scott, stayed home. He had no desire to sleep in a tent, even if it was just for two nights, or bounce all day in the back of a Jeep to glimpse animals he could see in the zoo. But he realized the trip was important to Eva and encouraged her to go. For Eva, sleeping in a tent—a new experience—and ballooning over the Masai Mara were the highlights of the trip. Awaking in the night to the noisy snorts of a hippo circling her tent was an experience she could never have at the zoo and one Scott would never want. "Ten years ago I would have been sorry he missed this trip. Now I'm grateful he missed it and so is he. Friends and relatives polite enough to sit through my slides of Africa have one of two reactions: 'Wow, I'd love to do that,' or "Wow, I'd never do that.'"

The point is this: a first-time skier lured down an "expert" slope will likely hate the sport forever. Likewise, if you're the type who would enjoy a safari or other adventure trip, encourage but don't push an unwilling spouse into the same mold. You could try gradual exposure to shorter, lighter adventure trips—a balloon ride over Napa Valley or a float trip down a scenic river, for example, in the hope that your sense of what's fun will gradually infect your spouse.

I Hate to Shop

Differences over daily activities can also surface on vacation. Problems develop when one traveler has no patience for shopping while his or her companion, who normally tires after five minutes of sightseeing, exhibits all the stamina of a marathoner when it comes to shopping. There are two potential sources of conflict here: how much *money* is spent shopping and how much *time*.

Couples can circumvent differences over shopping by agreeing in advance on the amount of time and funds to set aside for this activity. If you are in the habit of bringing home presents for family and friends, you can allocate an amount for each name on your list. This is particularly important if your budget is tight and your list long.

When Marco Polo brought home gifts from Asia, he may have unintentionally set an irreversible example. But in this "made in China" era, few foreign goods are so rare that we need to tote home a supply for everyone (with the exception of moon rocks, of course).

15

Certainly, you'll want to find that "surprise" you promised the children or Mom and Dad. But be careful. Once you start including your office staff, your spouse's office staff, nephews, nieces, Aunt Bessie and Fido, you may be setting a precedent you won't want to maintain. Not only can present hunting be costly, but it can absorb large chunks of your vacation time. Browsing in a new town can be fun, but racing around trying to find the right item for your gift list can be a drag.

On the other hand, if you love to shop but your spouse objects to the way you disperse joint funds, you can avoid dissension by BYOM—Bring Your Own Money—from your own birthday or allowance stash. That way no one can criticize your taste in elephant-hair bracelets or totem poles.

If it's the *time* your spouse objects to, shop while your partner sleeps in or does something else. One client's husband insists "absolutely no shopping" because he hates to waste his few vacation days on an activity he doesn't enjoy. He packs each day's itinerary full of sightseeing and cultural activities such as theater, ballet and concerts. Consequently, when his wife gets the yen to shop, she flies with girlfriends to Hong Kong or Paris for a few days.

You don't have to go that far with the girls. Most states have a few good cities for shopping. Los Angelenos, for example, can drive to Palm Springs, Carmel, Tijuana, San Francisco or Las Vegas for a change in stores. On the East Coast, the Big Apple is just a commuter train away from many states. Southerners can easily hop south of the border, while Toronto, Montreal and Quebec are a nice drive from New England. If these latter alternatives are too costly, you can always migrate downtown for a day.

I'm Not Going to Carry That

"Darling, can you squeeze my three pairs of new shoes in your suitcase? Mine is full."

"Sorry, honey, I don't have room. You should have thought of that when you bought them."

In this case, "Darling" is right. You'd better think before you buy. If your suitcase bulges before you leave home, you haven't left any growing room. My husband and I usually pack a small, soft duffel bag in one suitcase. As we accumulate purchases, we cushion any breakables with dirty clothes in the duffel bag. (You'll find packing tips in appendix A.)

The easiest way to handle purchases is to have the store ship them directly home. But there are disadvantages to this method. Retail stores generally charge for mailing and insurance, although sometimes the local taxes you save can cover the cost of the shipment. Also, you won't be able to whip out the Bavarian beer mugs for the office gang as soon as you get home. You'll have to wait two to eight weeks depending on how you shipped the merchandise. Unless you've made careful notes, by that time you may have forgotten who gets what. Finally, you run the risk that your selection will not arrive in one piece or be the right item.

Chances are, if you make your purchases at a store accustomed to tourists, you won't have to worry. Or, if on a tour, your guide can usually recommend reliable local merchants. In fact, it's not uncommon for guides to receive commissions from these merchants for directing tourists their way. By the way, if you have a problem with a foreign merchant, you can sometimes enlist the aid of that country's local trade commission to write a persuasive letter to that merchant.

Shipping from areas off the beaten track may not be easy or even advisable. When a descendant of Genghis Khan assures you that shipping the saddle you just bought from his tent in the Gobi desert is "no problem," don't count on it. In some developing countries, red tape or government fees make shipping unprofitable. In Mombassa, Kenya, I purchased 35 woven baskets at the request of a friend who collected them. The Peace Corps advisors at the crafts shop where I made the purchases apologized for their inability to ship the goods home—too many government forms and permits. Fortunately, another passenger on my flight home let me use part of her baggage allotment.

Although many air carriers count pieces, some still go by weight. My 20 pounds of excess baggage would have cost over $400 (much more than I paid for the bargains), equal to 1.5 percent of the highest normal one-way fare from Nairobi to Los Angeles.

The key, then, is to ask before you buy, How will I get this irresistible item home? For those traveling by chauffeur-driven limousine, tips to porters and excess baggage costs perhaps aren't a major concern. But if to save taxi fares, you board the airport bus laden with your camera case, hand luggage, purse, an 18" x 20" impressionist oil painting and a box of wine goblets from the Murano glass factory in Venice, you could be courting disaster. As you struggle to take your ticket out, oops—there go the goblets into the gutter. Your spouse gives you a look that asks, How could you drop $300 down the drain? and your otherwise perfect vacation takes a disappointing turn.

Even if you can cram your purchases into your suitcase, hauling 70 or more pounds around can be exhausting. It behooves you to pack light, and you may want to invest in lightweight, pliable luggage with wheels. Keep in mind that expensive, designer luggage is like an advertisement to thieves to "Come get me; I've got more goodies inside." Particularly when traveling to areas where theft is commonplace, you and your luggage want to keep a low profile.

ELIMINATING ANXIETIES

Another step toward harmonious travel with your mate is the elimination of anxieties. What anxieties? Not only the things *you*

18

worry about when you go on a trip but your spouse's concerns as well. Before you can eliminate these anxieties, you have to recognize them. Here are some of the common ones.

We're Going to Miss the Boat

Tensions frequently surface when one partner thrives on schedules and organization while the other is a "hang loose" type. One partner, for example, may have a chronic fear of missing the plane and the other may prefer to arrive at the airport five minutes before takeoff.

One businessman says he hates waiting around airports. It's a waste of his time. Since he bills his consulting time at $250 an hour, to him time is money.

His wife complains that this split-second timing makes her gray hairs multiply. "By the time we get to the airport, I've gnawed my $15 nail job to dust, and if we hit one red light too many en route, we have to fly like Superman down the concourse, pushing past people in the security check line and sweating through our brand-new travel clothes." Not the most relaxing way to start a vacation.

This fear of missing the boat/plane/train is one anxiety that can be eliminated by allowing the actual time normally required to arrive at your departure point plus 20 minutes for the unforeseeable: a late taxi, car trouble, traffic bottlenecks or hard-to-find parking at the airport. If you're driving yourself to an unfamiliar airport, add a 30-minute grace period in case you get lost.

One Friday evening, my husband and I started late for the airport. Our flight to Salt Lake City was the last one for the evening, and if we missed it, we'd lose our deposit on our accommodations in Park City. When we stopped suddenly en route to yield to an emergency vehicle, another car hit us from behind. We exchanged telephone numbers and insurance information with the other driver and sped off with 10 minutes to takeoff. At the airport, we jumped out of the car and found the trunk was jammed from the impact and we couldn't get our luggage out. Five more minutes ticked by until our pounding and pulling paid off. We sprinted to the gate in 80-degree weather laden with ski jackets and boots only to find our flight delayed an hour. That's why it's a good idea, when possible, to call the airline an hour or two before the scheduled departure to check for delays. Not only can you avoid unnecessary rushing but you'll also have time to select an epic novel to read when that hour delay grows into an epic three.

When you arrive at the airport "just in time" to catch your flight, you also run the risk of losing your reservation. Airlines routinely overbook and if you arrive late, you'll likely be one of those "bumped" and, if you arrive less than ten minutes before takeoff, you are not entitled to denied-boarding compensation from the airline. (International flights require more time.) Even if you manage to board late, your luggage may still be on a leisurely tour of the terminal. Some airlines make you sign a "late luggage" tag. Then if your bags don't make it to your destination, *you,* not the airline, pay for delivery. Airlines are adept enough at losing luggage; they don't need any additional help from you.

There is another side effect of late check-in. Many a client has complained, "We were supposed to sit together, but our preassigned seats weren't in the computer at check-in." Although little bugs in the computers occasionally mess up your seating, some airlines will give away your seat assignments if you don't check in at least 30 minutes in advance (one to two hours for international flights).

If you check in after those times, don't be surprised if some half-priced standby now has your aisle seat in the best location for movie viewing, while you are wedged in a middle seat between two kids prone to air sickness. It can be especially disconcerting on a 12-hour flight when a 300-pound stranger, whose deodorant isn't living up to its advertised stamina, falls asleep on your shoulder while your spouse is seated seven rows back. It's discomforting too when you have a bladder problem and must climb over three passengers and their full dinner trays to reach the aisle. Even if you are a "hang loose" type, your personality may turn from mild to mad when you get stuck with the seat that doesn't recline on a 17-hour flight to Asia. Instead of sleeping, you'll pass the hours mentally composing a strong letter of complaint.

Some airlines assign seats only at the airport. Since window and aisle seats in nonsmoking sections are most popular, late arrivals will get stuck with the undesirable seats.

I'm Afraid of Flying

One morning when the alarm clock failed, my husband and I missed our scheduled flight from Hyannis to Nantucket. We picked up a telephone marked "charter" in the airport and explained our predicament. A voice on the other end said someone would be right over. Fifteen minutes later, a baby-faced youth dressed in blue jeans introduced himself as our pilot. He didn't look more than 17 and the girlfriend he'd brought along for the ride looked even younger. We gulped and climbed into the four-passenger, single-engine plane, exchanging looks that seemed to say it had been a nice life while it lasted.

We flew in silence as if the sound of our voices might somehow upset the balance of the aircraft. In spite of a smooth flight, the thumping of our heartbeats competed with the drone of the motor and the 20 minutes seemed more like 40. We took the ferry back.

Risk-wise, airplane travel is still the safest way to journey. Nevertheless, there are times when even seasoned travelers have a twinge of the butterflies and think "what if," particularly during takeoffs, landings, turbulence and tornadoes. But that doesn't prevent them from accepting a small risk for the end result.

But what if you or your spouse has severe anxieties about flying? If your partner has a deep-seated phobia, there is probably little you can do without professional help except resign yourself to traveling without your love or taking a boat or train.

To someone with anxiety, a vacation may not be worth the intense fear while traveling. Fortunately, there are a few things you can do to help alleviate anxiety.

1. Take larger, multi-engine aircraft with a good safety record to your destination. The smaller the aircraft, the more aware you are of flying.

2. Take nonstop flights when possible.

3. Sit in the middle of the aircraft, away from the windows, where you can't watch the takeoff or landing.

4. As soon as you board, involve yourself in a book, magazine or conversation, so morbid thoughts can't command your attention.

5. Try to pick flights with a movie you haven't seen. Make sure it's not a disaster movie.

6. Avoid flying in winter when weather conditions are likely to be bad.

You're Driving Too Fast

"Slow down. You're following too close. Watch out! Don't pass now. We'd better stop before we run out of gas."

A driver bombarded with such ominous warnings from a "backseat driver" is apt to launch a warning or two of his own—something like "How would you like to get out and walk?" Road trips, even for couples who enjoy driving, can create a cacophony of criticism and defensive responses that sound worse than a broken muffler.

If your normally down-to-earth spouse fantasizes that he's Mario Andretti when behind the wheel, you probably sit in the front passenger seat, feet braced against the floor as if you could create drag and slow down the car. Unlike riding a roller coaster where "scared stiff" and "fun" are synonymous, there's no way to enjoy a road trip wide-eyed with white-knuckled hands gripping the seat. Given this scenario, you probably try to avoid road trips altogether. Sometimes, however, driving is the best way to explore a destination, and with a little restraint from both partners, anxieties, real or imaginary, can be eliminated.

A friend considers himself an excellent driver, but his wife has always been frightened by his aggressive driving style. Speed laws aside, he now reins in the horses when his wife is along. He discovered that "she's much better company when her heart isn't in her stomach."

On the other hand, if you're a chronic "backseat driver" no matter who's at the wheel, you're probably the one with the problem.

One woman I know drives an older, American-made station wagon while her husband drives a high-priced BMW with superior braking and cornering. When they travel together in his car, she mentally drives the car on the passenger side, her foot moving to an imaginary brake when traffic seems to warrant slowing. When her husband doesn't react at the same time, she reminds him, even through she's aware the car has better brakes. "I can't help watching the road," she explains, "except when I'm in a taxi or bus." In fact, she only has "backseat driver" syndrome when seated in the *front* seat. Her solution on longer trips is to sit in the back and put the dog in the front. It's not terribly romantic but easier on the nerves—both their nerves.

Sometimes the source of anxiety is not your spouse but Mother—Mother Nature, that is. Intense rain, blizzards, high winds, fog and icy roads can thwart even the most careful driver. You should try to anticipate and prepare for bad weather or roads, but sometimes the prudent action is not to drive at all until conditions improve. If you're driving to a ski resort, for example, you'll want to be sure your car, or the rental, has a windshield scraper, a working heater and defroster, antifreeze and snow tires or chains. Of course, if you don't know how to put the chains on, you'll be praying for a gas station to appear at the right time. Or if you abhor getting down under the car in wet snow when the chill factor is –20 degrees, you'd better rent a four-wheel-drive vehicle.

While some games can help pass the time on the road, there's one game that can cost you valuable time and sore feet. It's called "Guess how far we can get on our last gallon of gas?" Don't make your companion squirm for miles, eyes transfixed on the big *E* on the fuel gauge. Pull into a gas station with a comfortable margin in the tank and you'll avoid one more area of possible combat.

What If I Get Sick?

A man I know would love to travel, but his wife has bad knees and walking long corridors to the departure gates in airports can be painful. She rejects wheelchair assistance because, she says, "I don't want everyone staring at me." But I also know a young paraplegic who didn't miss a game run on the African safari he took with his parents. A client who's blind takes a cab to the airport and finds his flights. It's not uncommon to see sight-impaired skiers schussing down the slopes behind a guide at many resorts. There are even tours and cruises designed for dialysis patients.

In other words, few chronic ailments prohibit travel altogether. More often, they merely require the desire and additional planning.

For the woman with bad knees, the easiest solution would be a change in her attitude toward wheelchairs. But other alternatives include cruising, traveling by car or utilizing smaller, alternate airports where gates are only a few steps away from the entrance.

For some passengers, a bad back, hip or knee is aggravated by long periods of sitting in an airplane or car. Anticipating this problem, one couple breaks up transcontinental flights to New York or Boston with intermediate stops for a few days in San Antonio, New Orleans or Denver. This way they not only shorten the flight time of each leg but also have an opportunity to explore more of the United States.

If you're afraid of illness, a little preparation and common sense should get you through most situations. Obviously, if you or your mate suffers from angina, you won't be trekking in the Andes. Fortunately, that leaves a plethora of vacation spots around the world near good doctors and hospitals. The International Association for Medical Assistance to Travellers (IAMAT) publishes a booklet with the names and addresses of member doctors abroad (see appendix B). In major foreign cities, the United States Consulate can usually provide a list of American or recommended doctors in the area. If you have a medical problem that might require attention while abroad, having this list in advance could reduce fears about finding proper care.

The key, then, is to choose destinations and modes of travel compatible with your special health needs. After all, the possibilities of traffic accidents, influenza or food poisoning don't prevent us from going to work or school, visiting friends in the hospital, eating in restaurants or picking up a barbecued chicken from the market when we're too busy to cook. Why should such dark concerns dampen your travel plans? (Unless, of course, your doctor has advised against them.)

People in perfect health worry about getting sick too. A friend of mine twice planned a trip to Mexico and twice canceled. In each case, relatives just back from Puerta Vallarta or Acapulco described the ravages of "Montezuma's Revenge," in spite of staying in the best hotels and eating in the better restaurants. On the other hand, I've been to Mexico ten times and have never been sick. I have this unscientific theory that if you drink enough margaritas and eat enough hot sauce, you'll paralyze any germs. Fortunately, you can obtain a prescription for an antibiotic called Ciprofloxacin, which, when taken at the onset of symptoms, will squelch most routine diarrheal illnesses. Imodium A-D, available over the counter, can also calm the stomach.

A common fear for prospective ship passengers is seasickness. Your pharmacist can prepare a topical gel with scopolamine that can take the queasiness out of your cruise capers. And if you're a fair sailor except in heavier seas, over-the-counter tablets like Dramamine or Marazine provide relief on a temporary basis. They can make you drowsy and put a damper on your dancing, but at least you won't have to match your attire to the green of your face.

Remember to check with your travel agent for information on required shots and your doctor for any medications he or she deems appropriate for your destination.

My Spouse Snores

I was chatting with a friend in a department store about her upcoming trip to Europe when the sales lady at the counter blurted out, "I hate to travel." We both wanted to know why.

"I'm afraid of being left out in the cold," she replied. Hooked, we insisted on hearing her story.

She explained that she traveled with her husband once to a beach resort in the Caribbean. His loud snoring woke her up in the middle of a warm, balmy night, so she took her pillow and a blanket out on the balcony that overlooked the ocean and curled up on a lounge chair. She was awakened by the crackle of thunder. A cool wind was already whipping rain in her face and lightning flashed overhead. She jumped up to run inside, but the sliding glass door wouldn't open. She pushed and tugged, but it wouldn't budge.

Suddenly, the skies opened with a deluge. She pounded her fist on the glass and shook the door, but the sound evaporated in the rumble of the storm. She pounded for an hour before giving up. She sank into the rain-soaked chair and spent the rest of the night shivering in her soaking-wet nightgown.

When her husband unlocked the sliding door in the morning, he was surprised. "What are you doing out there?" he asked. "You're all wet!"

She was furious. "Why did you lock me out?" she demanded.

He explained that the wind woke him up in the middle of the night. He noticed the sliding door wasn't completely shut, so he got up and locked it, never even noticing that his wife wasn't in bed until the morning. That made her feel even worse. He spent the rest of the trip in the dog house; she spent the rest of the trip nursing a cold.

Some couples avoid traveling together because one of them snores. At home they may resort to separate bedrooms in order to sleep. But this arrangement can be costly when staying at hotels or cabins on a cruise ship. Obviously, one way to compensate for the extra room cost is to stay in less-expensive lodgings than you normally would, being content that a good night's sleep is worth any difference in room size or room service.

Sometimes the cost of a suite will be less than the cost of two separate rooms, particularly at all-suite hotels such as Embassy Suites, Hilton Suites and Doubletree Guest Suites, which feature a sofa sleeper in a living area separate from the bedroom. A suite at a hotel chain such as Marriott Residence Inns or AmeriSuites is usually more moderately priced than a simple room at a first-class hotel. The key is to be sure that the suite you book has a *complete* partition or door between the bedroom and living area. Don't assume that all the suites in a particular chain are exactly alike.

When cruising, look for ships that have at least one or two *single* cabins. These are priced almost 50 percent lower than double cabins. Otherwise, the rate for one person to occupy a cabin built for two can be up to double the per person rate. Multiply this cost times two cabins, and you could end up paying 100 percent more. You may need to book a year or so in advance because the few single cabins tend to fill up early.

In many cases, a snoring problem can be alleviated by one of several devices designed to ease breathing or sleep apnea. Consult with your doctor for the one most suitable for you and your traveling companion.

How Can I Leave the Kids, Mom, Dad, Grandma, the Dog, Aunt Betsy, the Plants, the Office?

I recently saw some clients I hadn't heard from in a long while. "Where have you traveled lately?" I asked.

"You must be kidding," the husband laughed. "We have two kids now."

While you may not want to leave a newborn or sick child, children don't have to mean the end of your traveling days.

One solution is to take the children with you (see chapter 6). The other solution is to leave them with someone you trust—a relative, a friend or a professional sitter. Of course this means additional costs and planning. Some zealous parents go so far as preparing and freezing the kids' dinners for every night they are away. Is the extra hassle worth the trip? If you have a good time, a good rest or a needed recharge of body batteries, it probably is. There are other benefits too. The children get to know their grandparents or cousins better, experience a different authority figure and have a vacation from their parents.

What about leaving Mom or Dad or Grandma if they're not in the best of health? If you don't have a reliable relative to look after your loved one while you're gone, hiring a professional nurse or companion is an alternative. You can leave a copy of your itinerary with the telephone numbers of the hotels where you can be reached if need be.

And what about your pooch, Fifi? You can board her at a commercial kennel, but chances are she'll get more tender loving care from a young relative or friend who can feed and walk your pet for some extra pocket change. The same person could pick up your mail and water your house plants too.

Fit these additional costs into your overall travel budget and pick a vacation and duration of stay according to the total cost. As for the extra hassle, once you have located and interviewed the babysitter or dog kennel for the first trip, you'll know whom to call upon the next time you travel, and planning will be easier. (See the travel checklist in appendix C.)

Another alternative is to make a deal with another couple you know. They can feed your dog, water your plants and look in on Grandma while you're gone, and you can feed their cat, pick up their mail and look in on Grandpa while they're gone.

"But I can't leave the office." This lament used to be reserved for husbands, but times have changed. With more women in business and the higher echelons of management, it's often both partners who must clear their calendars to break away from their respective offices. More and more, wifey is no longer readily available when hubby has the time to get away. Vacationing together takes advance decisions so replacements can be found, clients advised and unfinished business completed.

While many of us covet the notion that we are indispensable, somehow the office is still there when we get back. So what if "the mice will play when the boss is away"? Vacation is not, no matter how much we'd like it to be, a permanent condition. So relax and forget the office. You still have the other 50 weeks in the year to worry about it.

"But I'm the only one who can close a sale. When I leave, we lose sales and money." If you're convinced your special expertise will be sorely missed, consider beefing up your staff's training.

Obstetricians take vacations and babies are born anyway. Chief operating officers of international conglomerates take vacations. Even the president of the United States takes vacations. *You* can take a vacation.

NO RECRIMINATIONS, PLEASE

Almost nothing sours a vacation faster than useless recriminations. Blaming your spouse for the weather will not persuade the sun to creep out from behind rain clouds. Accusing your mate of loading the camera incorrectly will not reproduce your shot of the thousand-pound marlin that got away. When your partner loses the airline tickets, rubbing in the blame won't materialize a magic carpet home. Better to save your energy to solve the problem rather than haggle over it.

Once you agree on a destination, expect that some things will go wrong, mistakes will be made. (Mistakes can provide your biggest laughs later.)

Flexibility can make the difference between a trip that's successful and one that isn't. One couple returned from Europe with no desire to ever go back. Why? The airline lost their baggage for two days, the hotel was old, the weather in Nice was too cold for sunbathing on the beach and they took the wrong train.

Another couple returned from Europe but their similar tales had a different ring. When the airline lost their luggage, the concierge at their "wonderful old hotel" tracked it down for them. The weather was too cold for the beach so they rented a car and explored some "charming country towns." They took the wrong train and met a "lovely Dutch couple" who invited them to stay in their home.

In both cases, plans went awry but the second couple was able to "go with the flow" and make the best of the new circumstances. Even if your plans unfold with the precision of the changing of the guard at Buckingham Palace, that's no guarantee of a good time. Often, it's the spontaneous and unexpected encounters that create the most memories.

So when your spouse insists that Vienna is to the left and you dead-end at a canal in Venice, keep the "I told you sos" to yourself. It's a great exercise in self-discipline and part of the art of traveling with your spouse.

TWO

How to Travel with Your Lover

Advantages

A third of the couples whose trips I plan are unmarried. In many cases they've dated a year or more but sometimes only a month or two. Like traveling with a spouse, the chief advantages of traveling with your lover are companionship, shared experiences and an increased sense of security you don't have when traveling alone.

Beyond these benefits is the opportunity for couples to observe each other in a different environment, reacting to different stimuli, problems or tensions. Some couples see each other only under the best circumstances. Carefully groomed for dinner out or an evening of entertainment, each person is the object of the other's concentrated attention. But even couples who have lived together may experience a more intense test of their relationship the first time they travel together.

One young couple who visited Scandinavia broke up in Sweden and returned home separately. "I hate Sweden," the woman said when she returned to the travel agency with the unused portions of her ticket. "Too many beautiful blondes. My boyfriend flirted with every single one of them." She felt like "excess baggage" encumbering his pursuit of "wildlife." His feelings for her were shallow, she decided, especially when more attractive alternatives were around.

Another couple who had lived together three years returned from a week in Jamaica and immediately set a wedding date. Away from career and social commitments, they finally had time to assess their feelings for each other and plan for their future.

Just as a trip can flush out feelings, it can also illuminate attributes that may have been taken for granted or gone unnoticed. An attorney with political ambitions had taken his girlfriend to numerous fund-raisers and social events where he did all the talking and politicking. When the couple traveled to Europe, however, his girlfriend was the one with the more outgoing personality. Because she made friends so easily, they were invited into homes and to local events that most tourists never see. More importantly, the attorney was able to relax and let his girlfriend do the leading and organizing, abilities that he'd been too busy to notice at home. He realized she was one asset he wanted to hold onto for the long term and promptly fell in love—with a little help from the scenery on the Isle of Capri.

Which brings us to another advantage of traveling with your lover. While warm beaches and balmy nights combined with wine and song may not be essential ingredients for falling in love or staying in love, they are often the catalyst that speeds up the chemistry.

Disadvantages

Even couples who have been roommates may discover that togetherness is a little like pepper—interesting in small doses, irritating in large concentrations.

A teacher broke up with his girlfriend shortly after a trip to Hawaii. Although he had wined and dined her on home turf, it wasn't until they spent a week together that he realized how demanding she was. The hotel room had only a partial ocean view. She insisted on moving. The new room was too cramped. They moved again. Their table at the five-star restaurant was in the rear instead of by the window. She asked why he had neglected to tip the maître d'. The prime rib wasn't rare enough. The coffee wasn't hot enough. "I spent the entire trip negotiating with clerks, waiters and porters to correct imperfections," he reported. "I never had a chance to have fun." Although his girlfriend was beautiful and exciting, she was also, he discovered, spoiled and a chronic complainer. Nothing he did would ever be good enough. Although this realization may well be an advantage in the long run, it still ruined his only vacation of the year.

Sometimes, couples who travel together before they know each other well can misinterpret their companion's actions. A client accompanied a new boyfriend to Las Vegas while still in the middle of a divorce and couldn't get her mind off the proceedings. What had she neglected to tell the attorneys? What decisions had to be made regarding custody of her children? The divorce was all she could think about, yet she didn't share her worries with her new boyfriend because she "didn't want to involve him." She was not great company, but she could be. She'd often been the life of the party in the past, but her boyfriend never had that perspective. Interpreting her reticence as disinterest, he stopped calling her after the trip. In this case, traveling together may have caused the premature termination of a relationship.

Sometimes too, traveling together can create sexual pressure that neither person is ready for.

"No, you can't go to a weekend fraternity party," my mother insisted when I was a high-school senior dating a college freshman. "I know what goes on at those parties."

"But Mom, he hasn't even kissed me good night yet." I pleaded my case, but it was useless. It was a closed issue and stayed that way. I never did attend a fraternity weekend, but I did hear stories—stories that were still making the rounds at my twenty-year class reunion. What came through in many of these accounts was the awkwardness of not knowing what was expected of the young man or woman and the pressure to do what everyone else was doing. Instead of a new dimension in fun, some weekends withered into warlike maneuvers between couples.

Awkwardness is not merely a function of age or experience but of the relationship. A former classmate was thirty and had just broken up with a boyfriend when she was invited to a ski resort by a handsome advertising executive she had dated a few times. The mountain chalet they shared with two other couples had three bedrooms. Not quite over her last love affair, Susan opted for the couch. Because the other couples were sleeping together, she decided not to explain that she just wasn't ready for intimacy again and made up excuses such as "I think I have a cold coming on." It was an uncomfortable weekend and her last date with the man. "Who knows," she says looking back, "if I'd given myself more time to get over my old boyfriend before going on that ski weekend, that gorgeous hunk might still be around."

Sometimes the sexual pressure is on the man. A divorcee friend was invited for the weekend to the Palm Springs home of a businessman, also divorced. They had dated a year but their courtship had never "heated up." Linda anticipated the weekend away together would surely result in a closer physical relationship. When it didn't, all kinds of questions ran through her head. Was he gay? Just interested in her as a friend? Was he still in love with his first wife? Whatever the reason, the weekend was a disappointment.

For many, the invitation to "get away for the weekend" carries the implication of intimacy, which unrealized, can result in tension or even anger, especially when that expectation is what made the trip attractive in the first place. Since there's no travel insurance for smooth relations, it might be wise to temper such expectations with a generous dose of understanding.

Should I Go?

If you're unsure about traveling with your lover, or potential lover, questions to ask yourself include

- "How well do we know each other?"
- "How much do we like each other?"
- "What am I giving up?"
- "What am I gaining?"

A colleague had dated an attorney only a few times when he invited her to join him for a few weeks at his second home on Maui. "What do you think? Should I go?" she asked me. "He seems nice. I'd like to get to know him better, but I don't think I'm ready to . . . you know . . . get that familiar."

Gina's dilemma was not unusual. If this man had asked her directly, "Why don't you sleep over tonight?" her answer would have been a quick "No, thank you." Although divorced, she had no intention of rushing into an intimate relationship. But the same invitation, varnished with visions of moonlit palms and scented breezes, seemed somehow less brazen and more acceptable.

In the end, Gina answered her own question. She decided that accepting the offer would do them both a disservice. Accepting the invitation might suggest she felt more for him than she did, and since the main attraction for her was not the company but the destination, she decided to wait until she could afford to pay her own way. Then if any romantic feelings developed, she would know they were genuine and not a mere settlement of an IOU for a paid trip to Maui. She declined his offer with a request for a "rain check."

Another friend had different qualms about traveling with a boyfriend. She had a second boyfriend. If she went to Europe with Mark, what explanation would she give David? She didn't want to lie, and David wouldn't like the truth. She would be risking one relationship to develop another. Deciding that the offer in hand was better than one in the bush, she went to Europe. As a result, David disappeared from her life, and in spite of a wonderful trip, alas, so did Mark a short time after. Jackie is philosophical. "Mark didn't turn out to be Mr. Right, but the trip was worth it. I'll have a heap of memories for a long time." Now she's combing some old singles haunts hoping to run into David again "by accident."

SETTLE UP FRONT

Who Pays What?

A receptionist at a beauty salon asked me to arrange a ticket to Hong Kong. Her boyfriend, Frank, an apparel manufacturer, had invited her to accompany him on a business trip. Loretta had never been out of the country and was excited about the trip. Her boyfriend's ticket had already been purchased by his company while her ticket had to be paid seven days in advance for the best fare. When the deadline drew near, I asked Loretta about payment.

She told me to call Frank at his office. When I did, Frank responded that he would call Loretta and she would get back to me. We went around in circles with the question unresolved until the deadline had sailed like a Chinese junk into the sunset. "What ever happened to Hong Kong?" I asked Loretta the next time I saw her.

"It was all a misunderstanding," she explained. "Frank really couldn't afford to take me but was too proud to say so. He was waiting for me to offer to pay my own way. But the trip would have consumed my entire savings. Frank went by himself."

She was disappointed after all the planning and shopping she'd done for the trip and a little angry that Frank had been less than frank. "We're still friends," she added, "but do you know anyone who wants a good deal on a new set of luggage?"

Such misunderstandings arise when the question of who pays for what has not been answered in advance, usually because the couple is either uncomfortable with the subject or makes assumptions based on past experiences. If the boyfriend generally pays all expenses when the couple is together, the girlfriend may assume he intends to pay all trip expenses when, in fact, he has always split costs with traveling companions in the past.

It's a good idea to clarify up front which costs you'll pay separately and which will be shared. Be sure to include the following items in your discussion so they don't become stones in your shoes that constantly rub the wrong way:

1. Airfare, train, boat or car rental costs

2. Hotel bills

3. Meals

4. Tips, entrance fees, airport taxes, passport and visa costs

5. Personal items such as phone calls, dry cleaning, beauty salon, film

6. Shopping purchases

You can simply acknowledge which expenses you are willing to assume. For example, a woman whose boyfriend has invited her to meet his family in Little Rock could say, "If you're going to pay for my airline ticket, please let me take you and your folks out to dinner one night." Or if a fellow was invited to join his girlfriend at her family's condo in Aspen, he could volunteer, "Since we'll be saving on hotel costs, I'll be happy to treat you to dinner so you won't have to cook."

The rental of sports equipment can be costly. If the boyfriend is driving and paying the hotel bill, it might be the perfect time for the girlfriend to offer to rent her own ski equipment, golf clubs or scuba diving gear, purchase her own lift ticket or pay for her own tennis lessons.

On the other hand, if you have agreed to share expenses, you may want to make exclusions. "Sweetheart, a stuffed sailfish on my bedroom wall would clash with my collection of early Japanese erotica, so if you want to deep sea fish, it's out of your pocket," or "I'll split the hotel bill after you deduct the thirty-minute calls to your mother."

How minutely you track costs will depend on how you both settle such matters at home. It may be that the male partner always pays everything and it's unnecessary to itemize each expense. But if money is often a source of disagreement, you'll want to be sure blisters from those little stones don't fester into bigger sore spots.

You'll also want to think about who will receive the refund or bear any penalties if the trip is canceled.

A woman returned an unused ticket to me at the travel agency. She had broken up with her boyfriend prior to their planned ski trip and moved out of their shared apartment to her own place. She asked me to send the refund to her because the ticket had been her Christmas present. A check of the records, however, showed that her boyfriend had paid for the ticket with a company check. When I called him, he said he wanted the refund because his girlfriend owed him for a month's rent and telephone bill. I told the woman I was obligated to return the funds to the payee whose name appeared on the invoice and she would have to settle the "Christmas present" issue with him directly.

Sometimes, too, an individual may send a prepaid ticket to his love. If the couple breaks up before the trip, there is nothing—except ethics, of course—to prevent the recipient from using the ticket alone or cashing it in directly with the airline. If the ticket is refundable and has been paid by credit card, however, it can *only* be refunded to that card number. If payment was by check or cash, on the other hand, it can be refunded to the party whose name appears on the ticket, unless the "endorsement box" on the ticket carries a restriction such as "refund only to Silcatron Corp."

Advance-purchase fares and other airline bargain rates often carry penalties for cancellation or change. Penalties are also frequently imposed by cruise lines, tour operators, hotels and travel agencies. When arranging a trip, be sure your traveling companion understands these penalties. Agree in advance who will absorb the penalties in case your sweetie suddenly decides, "I don't want to go now. I gained five pounds and look lousy in my bathing suit."

You can insure yourself against trip cancellation charges but usually only for illness or death of a traveling companion or family member, having your home made uninhabitable, the default or failure of an airline or tour operator, or an accident that prevents you from reaching the airport. Trip cancellation insurance does not generally cover cancellations due to business or misadventures of the heart. Most travel agencies and some airports have trip cancellation policies on hand, along with baggage and life insurance.

When I went on dates as a teenager, my mother gave me "mad" money, just in case my date misbehaved and I needed a cab ride home. No matter how old you are or who pays for your trip, you should carry your own "mad" money so when you're in Pompeii and your relationship blows up, you can still get home.

One or Two Bedrooms?

Regardless of a couple's private relationship, one or both

partners may wish to present a platonic image publicly. A single parent, sensitive to the example set for a child, may feel more at ease with a separate room registered in his or her own name so telephone calls from home can be received directly. A sudden concern for public decorum may also surface when one individual takes the love of his life home to Sandusky to meet Mom and Dad. No matter that the lovers are in their forties. A sudden desire for separate bedrooms may merely reflect one partner's desire not to make the folks uncomfortable.

Given the added expense for the extra room, such concerns should be made known in advance to avoid a potential source of argument. Of course, if money is no object, you can reserve a two-bedroom suite and keep Aunt Betsy guessing about what you're up to. (If you can't afford separate rooms, you might have to invite Mom and Dad and little sis to visit you instead.) You may feel uncomfortable too if you're not registered as man and wife in foreign countries with more conservative mores. A young woman who traveled through a small town in Spain with her boyfriend reported poor service and looks of disapproval when the owner of a pension saw the different names on their passports.

In some places like Saudi Arabia, it's not only unacceptable for unmarried couples to stay together but also illegal and punishable by imprisonment. If you're uncertain about the customs or laws of another country, ask your travel agent or the tourist office representing that country.

No Strings Attached

Another question you may want to settle before you travel is what, if any, corollaries can be assumed from your trip together. Particularly when it's the first trip with someone, you may need to agree that traveling together does not imply any of the following:

- Exclusive courtship
- Engagement
- A proposal of marriage
- A decision to live together
- A declaration of love

Traveling together does imply that you expect to enjoy each other's companionship. If, as a result, your relationship takes a more serious turn, it can be a pleasant bonus. But a wonderful trip can lead to disappointment if the relationship is expected to reach a new plateau before you run out of clean clothes.

I met a fellow at a cocktail party who told me how he had taken a girlfriend to the Yucatan peninsula in Mexico. They had a fantastic time exploring the Mayan ruins at Chichén Itzá, sipping margaritas on the beach at Cancún and dancing into the wee hours. No problems. No quarrels. After they returned and had gone back to their respective jobs, he called the girlfriend to make plans for the weekend. She was busy. She was busy the following week too and the week after that. Soon she stopped returning his phone calls. He couldn't understand what happened. They'd had such a marvelous time together and she acted like she really cared for him. Now, like the mariachis and margaritas, she was gone.

I knew the young woman he was talking about. I had planned successive trips for her with different fellows. She was adventurous and loved to travel. And she always had a great time. But ready to settle down, she wasn't. It was obvious that when she sensed someone was becoming too serious, she would dump him without explanation. If she had warned her suitors in advance, perhaps the pyramid of broken hearts would not have rivaled the Temple of Quetzalcoatl. On the other hand, if she insisted on "no strings attached," she might never have been invited to places she was dying to see.

A little later at the party, I passed the same fellow with the "lost love" story. He was engrossed in conversation with an attractive woman with no ring on her finger. "The ruins are awesome," I overheard him say. "I'd love to show them to you. Why don't you go with me?"

Therein may lie his problem. Some people try to use travel as a means to a quick conquest. But like a roast cooked on high heat, the hearts in question may look ready on the outside while still untouched on the inside.

RISKS AND REWARDS

To Thine Own Self Be True

I heard a story about a bachelor who loved to sail. One day, while he was working on his boat, an attractive woman happened by. They struck up a conversation and she began to help him put the boat in tiptop shape. They sailed together down to Mexico and up to Canada. The sailor was thrilled to find a first mate who shared his passion for capturing the breezes. He proposed three months later. "On one condition," she told him. "First you've got to get rid of that goddamn boat."

The moral of the story? Travel can provide lovers with insight into each other's temperament, likes and dislikes but not if you disguise your true attitudes or personality in order to get along or impress each other. You may submerge your own identity for awhile, but sooner or later your real feelings will surface. The comfort seeker who loves luxury hotels will eventually turn thumbs down on those camping trips the adventurer loves. The beach bum will yawn when the culturist pitches the "Great Concert Halls of Europe" tour. The sooner you are honest about your interests, the sooner you can determine if such differences are important and how to work them out.

When You're Separated or Divorced

Unique risks exist for lovers who travel together when either is separated or the divorce is not final—risks that married couples don't have to think about. Sometimes, for example, separated spouses may attempt to reconcile and give their marriage another try. That's when their "in-between" experiences, like travel with another individual, can become a sore point. "You sure didn't waste any time taking your secretary to *our* hideaway. If you want me to move back in with you, you'll have to fire her first."

Even when a divorce settlement has been reached, expenditures can cloud the picture. "It's funny, Judge. Business is so bad, my ex can't pay the alimony he owes, but he just took his girlfriend to Tahiti. The only place he ever took me was Tijuana." In this case, the "ex" may find his trip to the South Seas carries costs not identified in the travel brochure.

Often, a separated couple will take a trip together to see if they can patch up their relationship or put the romance back in their lives. Travel expenditures for airline tickets, hotel bills and other costs can play an important part in establishing the legal date of separation. I was once called to testify that a separated couple had traveled together on a date much later than the husband was claiming as the actual date of separation. The fact that the husband paid for the trip and only one room was booked helped establish a later date of separation as claimed by the wife.

When You're a Single Parent

If you're a single parent who works, a decision to travel with a newfound love may present another conflict. Unless you're self-employed, chances are your paid vacation time is two or three weeks a year at most. This may mean less or no time to travel with your children. Your trip may also raise questions from a child like "Mommy, is that man you're leaving with going to be our new Daddy?" One father had a difficult time explaining to his teenage daughter why she could not drive from Los Angeles to San Francisco with her boyfriend. "Why not? You took your girlfriend to Hawaii and she's only a couple of years older than me," she kept insisting. I'm not sure who had the last word.

If child custody is still in contention, leaving your child behind while you travel with a lover could negatively affect your case. For a single parent, then, there's more to trip planning than deciding on an itinerary. Considering the possible side effects to your children is an important part of your decision making.

When One of You Has Medical Problems

Couples who vacation together are undoubtedly convinced they won't be sharing a disease. But if other medical conditions could interrupt your trip, it's just as important that your companion understand what problems could arise and be prepared to deal with them mentally, emotionally and even financially.

If you throw your back out at home, you can cancel a date and call your doctor. But on a trek to the midnight sun in Lapland, you and your companion may be stuck with each other "for better or worse," or at least until the next reindeer sled comes along.

How will your companion react if you become too sick to continue—with resentment because you're ruining the trip or with patience and helpfulness? What responsibilities can you handle if your partner becomes seriously ill? Do you have enough contingency funds with you to fly home immediately? Changing your original travel date can result in much higher airfares.

In an effort to put the best foot forward, couples may fail to fully inform each other about medical problems, allergies or required medications. Be sure you ask. Ask too for the name and telephone number of his or her doctor and closest relative. In this way, you're also letting your love know you expect the same kind of attention if you get sick.

Self-Renewal

For separated or divorced individuals, jumping back into the singles scene can be as traumatic as crossing a street in Paris. Coping with loneliness, feelings of failure and uncertain financial security can make travel an attractive escape from depression and an opportunity to recapture missed feelings of togetherness with a special someone.

Travel can also provide single parents, especially those who work, with some needed rest and time to themselves. Somehow, diverse cultures, exciting new cities and unfamiliar scenery have a way of sweeping us away from tedium and the bog of daily concerns, re-energizing our inner batteries with stimulating jolts to the senses.

I remember my first trip to Maui and the drive from Kahalui Airport to Kaanapali. The blue and turquoise sea splashed up along the palm-lined shore on one side of the highway. On the other, fields of lime-green sugar cane climbed into mountains and alternated with squares of red-brown earth, where the sugar cane had been burned for harvesting, sweetening the air with its intoxicating aroma. Rain clouds spilled over the summits like icing on a cake, and in the warm tones of the afternoon sky, a rainbow appeared, every hue from purple to yellow to red, brilliant and distinct. In those minutes, all else fell into proper perspective or retrenched into insignificance. And so travel can be its own reward, a fountain of renewal and source of unforgettable moments—moments made all the richer when shared with a love.

THREE

The Honeymoon

It Better Be Romantic

A honeymoon is more than part of the marriage rite. It's the realization of a private romantic dream shaped partly by movies, television, magazines, novels and stories from our parents, siblings and friends.

When I was a teenager, I cast every boy I liked into the same honeymoon scene that played in my imagination. We were walking along a beach in Hawaii at sunset while strains of the "Hawaiian Wedding Song" floated from a hotel terrace on whiffs of plumeria. As we stopped to kiss, my white chiffon dress fluttered in the sea breeze. My new husband was the picture of sophistication too, formally dressed in a tux, champagne glass in hand.

Only after I'd been to Hawaii did I realize there was something terribly wrong with this scenario. My honeymoon resembled one of those magazine ads where romance is linked with ownership of a luxury car. Only the Lincoln Continental was missing from the little movie in my head. Besides, no one dresses up in Hawaii. I was forced to revamp my honeymoon fantasy to be more in line with reality. (I think I transplanted it to Monte Carlo.)

Whether young or middle aged, by the time people marry, the honeymoon ideal has been kicked around in their imaginations and standards have been set, even if unconsciously, for the event. And it's a good thing too, because once the wedding date is set and the flurry of activity begins, there may not be much time to devote to honeymoon plans. Planning takes less time when you know what you like. It helps your travel agent, for example, if you know in advance that you always wanted to stay in a room with a heart-shaped bed and tub. That will narrow the alternatives immediately.

Whether your dream is sailing a small yacht through the Greek islands or staying in a historic house on Nantucket, whether it's your first marriage or your third, chances are you expect the honeymoon to be out of your ordinary routine and definitely romantic. But what if your spouse is not romantically inclined, at least by your definition? One groom's plans for a romantic honeymoon included frolicking on an isolated beach in Mexico, but his bride didn't want sand to ruin her $30 hairdo. When he suggested a hike down a tropical gorge to swim in a waterfall, she said her sandals hurt too much to walk that far. "Then how about a skinny-dip in the private pool at our honeymoon suite?" he coaxed. "Nah," she said. "Too many mosquitoes."

More often, however, it's the husband who is accused of having an unromantic nature. One honeymoon couple booked a seven-day Caribbean cruise. The bride, Jan, looked forward to romantic strolls on deck under the stars, dancing into the wee hours and exploring the lovely beaches at their island stops. But her husband, who loved to compete at games, chose the cruise to indulge two of his greatest passions—bridge and gambling. Jan did her best to lure him out of the bridge tournament and casino with hints of a passion of a different kind, all to no avail. Her marriage was only four days old, and already she felt like a nag.

After four days of frustration, she left her husband in the

casino for several hours. When he realized she wasn't around, he searched the ship and found her tangoing across the dance floor with one of the ship's handsome officers—a scene that aroused his competitive spirit. He made sure Jan's next dance was with him and then led her outside.

"What were you doing with that guy?" he demanded.

"You know how I love to dance," she told him, "and I didn't want to disturb you when you were having such a good time in the casino."

He could hardly be angry when she had been so considerate, so he kissed her and she finally got her romantic stroll on deck under the stars.

It's been said that the first year of marriage is the toughest because couples are just learning what's important to their partners. Sometimes it takes very little to make your partner happy—a couple of dances, a couple of kisses, a few good trump at bridge. Make sure your honeymoon includes time for what your love expects from you as well as what you expect. After all, it's a heady feeling to know you're capable of fulfilling someone else's dreams.

What's Romantic, What Isn't?

Just as there are universal ideas of what constitutes romantic music, a romantic movie or even a romantic novel, there are generalizations about what constitutes a romantic honeymoon. While it takes two to create this recipe and no scientist can tell you the exact ingredients, there are some general guidelines to what's romantic and what isn't.

Sex is an important component. For some couples, sex may be all that's necessary to make the trip memorable. Even couples who have lived together a year or more generally expect reaffirmation from their new spouse of their desirability. So anything that interferes with sex is unromantic.

Sickness, for example, is unromantic. If the bride packs a flu bug along with her most enticing negligee, not only is she unlikely to feel enthusiastic about lovemaking, but her husband won't be anxious to share her sore throat and upset stomach either. How can you stay healthy on your honeymoon? Sometimes you can't. You can't help it if Aunt Betsy, who trekked from subzero Kalispell for your wedding, hands you a touch of bronchitis along with your wedding present. You can't prevent all those long-lost kissing cousins from passing their colds down the reception line anymore than a security check can prevent undocumented germs from circulating in the airplane cabin on your eight-hour flight to Tahiti. But you can take a few steps that will increase your chances of staying healthy.

If possible, *don't* rush off on a long flight (long is anything over two hours) the night of your wedding. It's one thing if the wedding is over in the afternoon, but leaving your wedding at 10 P.M. for a night flight from San Francisco to Miami so you can transfer to a ship for a 5:00 P.M. sailing to the West Indies means you'll be up for two days with no sleep. Unless, of course, you're contortionists who can sleep on a plane in spite of the fact that your knees are under your chin.

The last days before a wedding can be hectic. Between bachelor parties and rehearsal dinners, visits with out-of-town guests and stress from relatives who want *your* wedding done *their* way, chances are you've had less sleep than usual even before the ceremony. Instead of compounding the exhaustion with a night flight, you can check into a local first-class or deluxe hotel for a rest night. Be sure to inform the staff that you're a honeymoon couple. Some hotels offer a honeymoon package that consists of a suite or mini-suite with a king-size bed and bottle of champagne for a little more than the regular double rate. While few hotels will guarantee the type of bed available on a given night, the word "honeymooners" will emphasize the importance of a queen-size or king-size bed, and generally, most hotels will do their best to give you a large bed if possible. (Sharing a twin bed can be romantic but uncomfortable.) Naturally, you won't leak the hotel name to your practical joker friends unless you want to find the bed short-sheeted or worse.

If you have a flight the next morning, consider staying at a hotel near the airport the first night so you can sleep a little longer. Avoid a 7 A.M. flight departure, which really means getting up around 5 A.M. to able to check in by 6 A.M. Lowered resistance due to lack of sleep is one illness factor you can control.

Sunburn can interfere with sex too. There's nothing romantic about kissing your sweetheart and hearing "Ouch!" instead of a pleasurable sigh. Sun-block lotions and cover ups can help make sure your outdoor activities don't interfere with your indoor activities. After all, what's more important on this trip?

Two clients went skiing on their honeymoon. They were both excellent skiers, but the husband took a hard fall and dislocated his shoulder their first afternoon on the slopes. While he could have slipped on the ice going to the market with the same results, the fact is that even after they were tired, he wanted to "bomb down one more run." Whether your sport is tennis, swimming or skiing, the idea is to pace yourself, quitting sooner than later. Playing too hard can keep lovebirds a plaster cast away.

Another important aspect of the romantic honeymoon is saying the right words—words like "I love you," "I'm so lucky to have met you" or "I'll love you forever." They don't have to be original, only sincere. You're not competing for the best script, just the best heart. Cliché or not, the frequent profession of love and acknowledgment that you made the right choice can lift any trip out of the mundane into the memorable.

Unromantic are words like "Can't you read the damn map?"

"We missed our turnoff" or "How could you miss that ball, it was right in front of your racket?" The word "honeymoon" implies that the first month of marriage is the sweetest. You'll have a lifetime to criticize each other, so why start now?

The honeymoon is also a time when you expect to be the sole object of your spouse's attention. Sharing the Jacuzzi at sunset is romantic. It's not romantic if the bride sits there alone while her husband is glued to the television in their room for hours of football. Likewise, it's unromantic to gawk at another attractive man or woman, even on the topless beach at St. Tropez, when your new mate is talking to you.

Does that mean the ideal honeymoon spot is a remote island with thatch-roofed huts where the two of you can feel like Robinson Caruso? Not necessarily.

Each year, thousands of honeymooners select just that kind of seclusion, perhaps with a few more amenities, at Caribbean islands like St. Croix in the Virgin Islands, Turtle Island in Fiji or Young Island in the West Indies. And that's fine if you are relaxers whose favorite entertainment is sleeping, reading, swimming, snorkeling, sunset watching or mai tai sipping. If not, you could develop a quick case of island fever. One does not live by love alone. No matter how much two people love each other, there's only so much you can do to entertain each other without a little outside help from nightclubs, restaurants or sports activities. If you're quick to get restless, it would be wise to balance your trip with a destination that offers options such as sightseeing or shopping.

For example, if one of you is a relaxer and the other a travel enthusiast, you could balance three days of shell searching on remote beaches with a few days of shopping and dancing in a city. Otherwise, you may find that even a beautiful paradise like Bora Bora in French Polynesia can be boring-boring.

Romantic Atmosphere

Is one place more romantic than another? A couple from northern California arranged their wedding atop the Temple of the Seven Dolls at the ruins of Dzibilchaltun in the jungles of the Yucatán. Afterward, they bathed, along with their friends, in a 140-foot-deep sacrificial well before moving on to a more conventional tub at a deluxe hotel in Mexico City. Definitely memorable. Certainly original. And, from the couple's viewpoint, absolutely romantic.

You don't have to go that far (or that high) to find romantic atmosphere. In fact, individuals who don't fair well in high humidity and intense sun might find the Yucatan too hot to get close to each other.

While tropical settings in places like Mexico, Hawaii or Jamaica are popular choices for newlyweds, balmy weather and lush foliage are not the only definitions of romantic atmosphere.

"Romantic" is a mood that can be captured in variant environments. Romantic can be an evening's stroll through the Bavarian-like village of Vail, Colorado, where snowflakes pirouette in the gleam of twinkling lights that frame rooftops and windows, the jingle of laughter spills out the doors of restaurants and bars into the crystal air, and healthy faces glow with exhilaration from the day's physical challenges.

Romantic can be New York, when sidewalks, rinsed by a sudden thunderstorm, sprout crops of colorful umbrellas and shoppers are sent scurrying for cover amid the clatter of hawkers and taxi horns.

Or it can be San Francisco when the fog tiptoes across the Golden Gate bridge and plays hide and seek with sleek skyscrapers, while fog horns bellow greetings from the bay.

Romantic is not so much the scenery or weather as your point of view. The feeling inside when you're with the person you love is like having a pair of rose-colored glasses that permits you to shape and color the ambiance around you.

Romantic can be almost any place devoid of weather extremes—fog or blizzards that keep you holed up in an airport for eight hours, hurricanes that threaten your life or property, intense cold, intense heat or whatever makes activity impossible or uncomfortable for you. Extreme weather can't always be predicted but you can avoid places that are notorious during certain seasons. If you have to fly out of heavy weather in the northeast or midwest in winter, for example, try to take nonstop flights. Delays due to weather tend to be compounded with each additional connection point. Avoid the Gulf Coast during hurricane season, or at least be prepared to move fast. Avoid safaris during the rainy season and India in August.

Consult a travel guidebook for the usual weather patterns at a given destination, or ask your agent, keeping in mind he or she is not clairvoyant and has no special access to the whims of Mother Nature.

SIDESTEPPING SNAFUS

Insufficient Funds

It's not easy to anticipate how much money you'll need, particularly if the honeymoon is your first trip together. Failing to come close, however, can be disastrous.

An attorney just starting his own practice had $2,500 to spend for his honeymoon. He picked a deluxe resort in Hilton Head, South Carolina, just a few hours' distance from where the couple lived in Columbia. The hotel would cost $150 a night, but this would still leave a comfortable margin for meals, recreation, transportation and entertainment.

His bride, however, had her heart set on Hawaii and selected a seven-night economy package at a condominium. Although the air-fare and hotel already totaled $2,000, she figured they could save on meals by dining in, and they could rent bicycles and sightsee on their own. What she didn't figure on was rain. It rained too hard for biking so they rented a car. With gas, tax and insurance the rental cost over a hundred dollars. Food at the market was more expensive than anticipated. The rain also limited the free outdoor activities and the couple had no money left for shopping or indoor entertainment. Although they made it home with a few dollars left, they had spent a large part of their vacation counting every penny. Instead of relaxing, they worried about stretching their dollars. The shortage of funds dampened their spirits more than the rain.

A friend of mine remembers her honeymoon vividly. She and her husband drove more than five hours to a California ski resort after their ceremony. Neither had a credit card, but they planned to pay for accommodations with personal checks. The lodge would not accept checks, however, and insisted on credit card payment or cash.

The couple stayed one night and drove the next day several hours south into the desert, where the only available hotel would not accept checks without credit card identification.

Once again, they packed up and moved on to Las Vegas. They found a motel that would accept their check but had no restaurant. By that time, they were short of cash for meals. With 55 cents left in their pockets, they didn't eat for 24 hours and left the next day, fingers crossed that their last tank of gas would hold out until they got home. Their one-week honeymoon had been reduced to three days of driving, packing and unpacking. From then on, and until they qualified for credit cards, they made it a habit to carry traveler's checks. In spite of the feeble honeymoon, the marriage is still going strong.

If you don't possess a credit card, have a low credit limit or don't want to carry a lot of cash, consider prepaying hotel accommodations and all tour or transportation costs. This will free up your cash for meals, fun or unexpected expenditures. By doing so, however, you may be trading away some flexibility. If you're not happy with the hotel you've selected or wish to leave a destination early, you may have a harder time getting your money refunded. Or, if you're forced to cancel, you could lose more than the one-night deposit you normally would have invested. Be sure to investigate the hotel's cancellation policy in advance and ask your travel agent to include that information on your itinerary.

Another couple picked an isolated village in Baja, Mexico, for their honeymoon. They wanted a small, quiet, unsophisticated place to unwind. Between them, they were armed with five major credit cards. All of them proved useless because the charming but small, quiet and unsophisticated hotel did not accept credit card payment. Although they had some cash in hand, this couple too was forced to cut short their vacation. Particularly when traveling outside the United States, check the hotel's policy on payment or ask your travel agent.

It's best if you carry various forms of payment to cover every situation: credit cards for major expenses like hotel, car rental and meals; traveler's checks for situations where credit cards are not accepted; local currency for taxi cab drivers and small vendors who lack the means of changing money; and U.S. dollars when they can wangle the deepest discount, best rate of exchange or biggest smile from a bellman or waiter.

If you're relying on credit cards for a large percentage of your expenditures, don't use up your limit to purchase airline tickets or clothes for the trip prior to traveling. If you do run up charges, send a check to the credit card company in advance of your trip. Otherwise, you might feel your face flush at the Ritz in Paris when the waiter says, *"Je regrette, monsieur, que votre carte de crédit est . . .* how you say . . . no good."

Rough Relations with the Ex

When the bride or groom has children by a previous marriage, the ex-spouse may play a part in the honeymoon plans, particularly if the relationship between exes now resembles that of the cartoon duo Tom and Jerry—each out to do the other in.

A honeymoon couple emphasized that whatever arrangements I made for them should be kept top secret and communicated only to them. They feared the groom's ex-wife would mess up their plans—cancel their hotel reservations, call them daily about money matters and indulge in other forms of harassment—if she heard about them from the kids.

The former wife's attorney reminded the groom, however, that according to their divorce agreement, the ex-wife had a *right* to know how to get in touch with him in case an emergency arose with the children in her custody. And the groom shared the concern that he be reachable in the event of an emergency. But how could the honeymoon couple protect their privacy if the ex-wife had a copy of their itinerary? They solved the dilemma by announcing that they were driving through New England and "playing it by ear." Since they didn't know what town or inn they would end up in each evening, the groom would call his children and check in along the way. He scheduled his telephone calls for the morning of check-out from each location. That way he knew the kids were okay, and if his ex made any crank calls, it would be too late to do damage because he had already left. Fortunately, the new bride understood that some of their trip time would be devoted to calls to the ex-family and that the second-time-around honeymoon would not be like the first—free of outside responsibilities. Particularly when children are involved, the ex-wife or ex-husband is often a factor to be reckoned with, even on the honeymoon.

Honeymoon with Ma and Pa

Most people's fantasy of the perfect honeymoon does not include reservations for four. Yet there are times when, for the sake of peace in the family, Mom and Dad have to be included somewhere in the itinerary.

A couple who lived in Los Angeles were married in Las Vegas. It was the second time around for both of them. Both sets of relatives were scattered across the United States and the wedding became a de facto family reunion. It was also an opportunity for the families to get to know each other at the blackjack tables and cocktail shows. After the wedding, the couple stayed in Las Vegas to share the fun and show all a good time. They had a ball together, partly because the bride and groom were already comfortable enough with each other to deal with their families' anxieties over meeting for the first time.

Then too, both partners had been on an alone-at-last honeymoon after their first marriages, and they didn't need to fulfill that particular fantasy again.

For other families, a few hours together requires a monumental effort in diplomacy. Mediating relations among relations places an unnecessary strain on the new couple, especially with nerves already on edge for the wedding.

So what do you do if Ma and Pa journey all the way from Auckland, New Zealand, for your wedding in Macon, Georgia? You can't just say, "Thanks for coming, you all." One option is to ask your folks to come in advance of the wedding so you can all spend time together before the ceremony. But sometimes entertaining your parents while trying to prepare for the wedding and honeymoon is like plugging frazzled nerves into an electric socket. One bride, exhausted from running her folks around to all the local sights, developed bronchitis and the groom almost developed cold feet. An alternative is to suggest that after the ceremony, Ma and Pa sightsee a little on their own, and after you've been on a short honeymoon, you can all spend more time together.

Honeymoon with the Kids

While most of us think of a honeymoon as a vacation built for two, there are no fixed rules as long as the bride and groom are in agreement.

When Robert Louis Stevenson married a divorcee, Fanny Van de Grift Osborne in 1880, he was 29 and she was 42. After the ceremony, they honeymooned in a rustic cottage in the wine country of Sonoma, California, along with Fanny's twelve-year-old son, Lloyd. For its time, it was an unconventional honeymoon for an unconventional couple. Yet it was there, while vacationing on the slopes of Mount Saint Helena, that Stevenson drew the inspiration for *Silverado Squatters* and the classic children's tale *Treasure Island*.

A friend recently took his eleven-year-old daughter on his honeymoon. During his two-week vacation each year, she would travel from Montreal to visit him in Dallas and he could not afford additional time off for a separate honeymoon. While the couple would have many weekends to be alone together, this trip was the only opportunity for the bride and stepdaughter to get to know each other.

Another couple each had children by former marriages who joined them on their honeymoon. In the relaxed atmosphere of a beach resort, the kids got to know not only their respective new stepparents but their stepsiblings as well. Caution: Even when travel arrangements turn out perfectly, relations may not be harmonious, especially if the children haven't fully accepted your marriage. If you're unsure how the kids will react, bringing them along could be risky business.

Delayed Honeymoon

A friend married on a Sunday evening and arose the next morning at seven o'clock to go to work. When she and her husband were able to break away from their jobs a few weeks later, they flew to Vancouver, Canada, for a long weekend. That first trip together as newlyweds became their honeymoon.

For some couples, the honeymoon is postponed for months or even years. But even if a couple has never had a honeymoon, they can still plan one.

A friend who got tired of waiting for a honeymoon kidnapped her husband from work the day before their fifteenth anniversary. Sworn to secrecy, his colleagues were informed in advance so they could cover for him at work. His wife had packed his suitcase and she drove him straight to the airport before he had a chance to protest. Because he was a country-western music fan, she had made arrangements to fly to Nashville to see the Grand Ole Opry and soak up "that country feeling." He loved it.

While you may not feel the excitement and anticipation of that first night of marriage, you may still capture romance on your 10th, 25th or 40th anniversary. Just realize how lucky you are to have each other. Turn on your enthusiasm, your smiles, your favorite music and think romantic. Fortunately, it's never too late for a honeymoon.

FOUR

How to Survive Traveling with Your Boss

Advantages

The president and the vice president of a California software company were talking at a dinner party about their recent trip to Boston to close a merger with another firm. Another dinner guest asked Bert, the vice president, if the meetings had been easy or tough. Bert laughed and pointed to his boss. "You'll have to ask Jeff. I didn't have much time for meetings. I was too busy getting his suit pressed, sending faxes and shopping for the other executives' wives."

"Your *shopping* almost ruined the deal," Jeff countered. "You see," he explained to the other guests, "I asked Bert to buy a little present for the wives to give them at our closing dinner. Guess what he bought? *Surge suppressers.* Here are nine senior ladies, all dressed very elegantly, thanking us in advance for our thoughtfulness, and then they pull out these floor plugs. I wanted to die of embarrassment."

"You have to admit they were nicely wrapped," Bert responded tongue in cheek. "Besides, my background in systems engineering didn't prepare me for shopping. Next time you can do it."

"Next time," Jeff winked, "I'll take your secretary and you can stay home."

"That'll be my pleasure," Bert joked.

Whether traveling with the boss is an advantage or disadvantage depends somewhat on your expectations about traveling together.

"I want you to fly to Dallas with me tomorrow to pitch a new account," your boss says. Even when that invitation is last minute, it's not one you can easily refuse, unless you're collecting pink slips to make a collage. And why would you refuse when there are advantages to traveling with the boss, including the opportunity to know each other better?

Any rapport you build outside the office will likely carry over to your job. Then if it comes to promoting you or someone the boss doesn't know as well, you'll probably be the one to uncork the bubbly. Similarly, during a staff cut, a personal rapport with the boss can make the difference between who goes and who stays.

A trip with the boss can also provide insight into the company's direction and your place in its future. Busy with their work, both boss and employee may have little time during office hours for off-the-cuff communication or airing grievances in a relaxed, informal way. On a three-hour flight, however, you'll have a captive audience for your new idea on how to increase profits or promote the latest product.

Traveling with the boss can also prove an important learning experience. Observing how a deal point is negotiated, a problem solved or advice dispensed can be excellent training. And if the boss is not so successful in these tasks, you can learn what mistakes to avoid. Even if the trip reaps no business rewards, the opportunity to familiarize yourself with another city and its hotels and restaurants will help make you a well-seasoned traveler.

Disadvantages

If your boss qualifies for your "least favorite person" award, you can usually find ways to avoid interchange at the office. You can place those requested files on the chief's desk when he or she steps out of the office and frequent lunch spots you know the boss loathes.

It's not so easy to avoid each other on the same flight or to bow out of dinner together with clients. You'll have to spend more time—or waste it, depending on your viewpoint—with the boss than usual. Some companies insist that staff members take separate flights to the same destination. That way, if a crash occurs, the loss of expertise to the company will not be compounded. If the prospect of conversing with your boss for more than five minutes throws you into depression, suggest that you take separate flights in the interest of protecting the company from a double loss. Of course, if your boss is a vintner and you're a grape stomper, that argument won't hold wine. If desperate, you can always take a Dramamine or drink a double martini and feign unconsciousness for the entire flight.

Traveling with the boss can also spoil you. Some company travel policies insist that employees travel regular coach or on discount fares unless they are traveling with the boss, in which case, they both go first class. With the boss, an employee might overnight in deluxe hotels, ride in chauffeur-driven limousines and dine in award-winning restaurants. The employee then feels let down when these privileges disappear. Sometimes it's left to the travel agent to bring the traveler back to earth.

"Coach? Last time I went first class."

"Sorry, Mr. Peters, our instructions from your company are to book you in coach, and you'll have a subcompact to drive to your economy motel."

"Subcompact? I'm six feet five!"

"Sorry, Mr. Peters, our instructions—"

"Well, how much is first class? Maybe I'll pay the difference myself."

"Two thousand dollars."

"Uh, let's hold off. Maybe I can get out of going on this trip."

After traveling first class, the employee may resent the step down in luxury and cause friction with the powers that set the company travel policy.

Another disadvantage of traveling with the boss is that unless you have already established bonds of trust with each other, you may be ill at ease and watchful of remarks you make about colleagues or superiors that could filter back to the office out of context. If you avoid rendering an opinion, you can look like a dunce. Rendering one honestly but diplomatically, however, is an art, especially after a bottle of wine with dinner. Some bosses like to play devil's advocate. They appear to have a negative opinion about some person or issue to provoke positive arguments. Afraid of developing a case of "foot-in-mouth" disease, you may feel too inhibited to speak freely.

Another disadvantage is that you'll probably have to modify your schedule to accommodate the boss. An analyst who worked for a developer liked to swim laps, jog or work out after work each day. On a business trip, however, he had to pass up the inviting health club at his hotel to accompany his pudgy boss to dinner followed by an exploration of the local night spots.

Then too, it's the boss's calendar that takes priority and when you're told to leave at 5 P.M. Wednesday for Cincinnati, too bad if you'll miss your wine-tasting class or your cousin's birthday party.

WHEN THE BOSS WANTS TO SAVE MONEY

Sharing a Room

While most companies accommodate their traveling staff in separate rooms, smaller businesses may not have that discretion.

A client who earns commissions from the sale of large manufacturing equipment usually doubles up with his technicians in the same hotel room. If he closes a sale, the cost of travel is covered, but if he comes home empty-handed, the travel expense is a personal loss. It's understandable in such cases why the boss may ask an employee of the same sex to share a twin room.

According to the *Wall Street Journal,* the former president of Wal-Mart, one of America's most successful companies, attributed its earnings success to 10-hour days, six-day weeks and executives sharing hotel rooms.

If you're an individual who values privacy or loathes sharing a room with a boss whose habits you abhor, you can offer to pay for your own room with the explanation that you're a closet smoker or that your snores rattle a room like the Brooklyn subway. Your willingness to dig into your pocket telegraphs two things: you're serious about your own room and you have the budget interests of the company at heart. Often when you demonstrate such consideration, the boss is motivated to respond similarly and bend to accommodate your wishes.

Staying Longer to Save on Airfare

Have you ever wondered why you paid $500 more than the passenger sitting next to you for the same trip to New York? You eat the same microwave chicken, watch the same movie and sit in identical seats.

Airfares are designed to lure stay-at-homes to travel with lower round trip rates that often include advance purchase requirements and restrictions on the length of stay. These lower fares are often subsidized by higher fares imposed on the business traveler who wants to be home by Friday night.

Since most discount fares not only require passengers to book in advance but also to stay at the destination over a Saturday night, some companies book return flights on Sundays. The airfare savings may keep the sag out of the bottom line, but a weekend with the boss can play havoc with your home life. If you're a married female traveling with a male boss, for example, you could have a difficult time convincing your husband that Saturday night in Honolulu is "strictly business." The boss's wife may regard you with suspicion too. On the other hand, if you're single, you might even enjoy the extra time out of town.

Business emergencies, client meetings, seminars, product shows and conventions don't always occur at the most convenient times. When accepting a job that requires travel, it's best to discuss your particular parameters up front. Make it known then that you expect travel not to interfere with your weekends with the family. Even then, the company's needs and your job responsibilities can change along the way. In the end, if your boss proves inflexible, a choice between family and career may be unavoidable.

Driving to Avoid Airfare

Unless you love to drive, business travel that requires road trips longer than three hours can be grueling. Even when you trade driving shifts with the boss, sitting in a car for six hours can tire you out; aggravate knee, back and neck problems; and spoil your humor, especially if you know a flight would get you there in 50 minutes with fewer wrinkles in your clothes and forehead.

In this era of deregulation, many small cities lack convenient air service and driving may be the only way to reach certain destinations. Your company, however, should be willing to fly you to the closest airport so your drive in a rental car will be as short as possible (three hours maximum). So, if the boss wants to drive the 382 miles from Los Angeles to Sacramento, point out that the wear and tear on his car might eventually cost more than the airfare, unless, of course, numerous business stops need to be made along the way.

If you tend to get sleepy driving over 45 minutes and no amount of coffee, blaring music or wind rushing through the windows can keep your eyelids from feeling like lead weights, ask the boss to stay awake when you drive. Fear of your going catatonic at the wheel could be just the just the incentive the boss needs to purchase airline tickets.

On the other hand, a road trip can be enjoyable if the time is broken up with stops and overnights along the way. Misery sets in when, instead of knocking off at 6 P.M. to rest up at a motel or hotel, you push on all night to get to the next city. A considerate boss won't ask you to do that unless you're the lead guitarist in the band and you missed the last flight to the gig in Biloxi.

Confiscating Your Airline Awards

From time to time, airlines offer perks to passengers for flying with them. If, for example, you are a frequent flyer on Magic Carpet Airlines, the miles you fly may earn you coupons good for free hotel nights, car rentals, first-class upgrades or even free tickets for domestic and international flights.

An attorney with a national corporation frequently accompanied the firm's officers on business trips. Over two years, he earned enough mileage points to take his family on a free trip and casually announced his intentions to the boss.

The chief, however, said that because the corporation had paid for the travel that earned the awards, the free tickets should be used only for corporate travel.

The attorney thought of his wife and two kids who were already packed for Asia. "But I'm the one who has to get up at 5 A.M. for a 7 A.M. flight, forego dinner with my family for airline grub and spend hours waiting in terminals for connections. The mileage awards are my compensation."

"Sorry—company policy," the chief insisted.

Such a policy, however, is difficult to enforce without the cooperation of the traveler. Keeping track of mileage credits can be like keeping track of paper clips, consuming more staff hours than the savings accrued to the company.

The business travelers I've known who routinely give their awards back to the company tend to have one thing in common: they are in the upper income brackets and can easily afford personal travel without mileage awards. But as one chief executive officer put it, "Even if the policy isn't totally enforceable and only half-effective, the savings can still be reflected in the annual report."

Other chiefs, however, don't believe the savings would outweigh the loss of an effective but disgruntled employee. They feel that allowing travelers to keep their mileage awards for personal travel is a low-cost way for the company to be a hero.

If you're a frequent business flyer who looks forward to using airline awards for next year's trip to China with the family, be sure you understand your company's policy before you find yourself up the Yangtse without a chopstick.

I've also known frequent flyers who would rather connect twice on their mileage airline than travel nonstop on another, just to collect points. "What's the difference," they ask, "as long as the airfare isn't higher than the company would normally pay?" But cost can be measured in time too—the extra time out of the office for the longer flight route and the time out for the traveler to recuperate and perform at peak efficiency.

Just as employees expect to reap the rewards for their travel time, companies expect that their corporate travelers won't pile up mileage points at the expense of the company. Of course, sometimes it's the boss himself who, to collect mileage, insists on connecting through Atlanta on the way home to Los Angeles from Seattle, even though your mileage-credit airline flies nonstop and would get you home two hours earlier. You can try reason, but don't be surprised if the response is "I'm paying. We'll do it my way."

WHEN THE BOSS WANTS TO SAVE TIME

Taking Night Flights

Time out of the office for travel can mean lost sales and inefficiency or overload on other personnel left in the office. Even if your trip with the boss represents a brief escape from a paper jungle, the short-lived peace can be deceptive. Like crocodiles in muddy rivers, the stack of unattended backlog lies in wait, ready for attack upon your return.

Some business travelers in the West reduce time out of the office by taking the "red-eye," a flight that leaves around midnight to arrive at East Coast cities at 6 or 7 A.M. local time, allowing a full day's work. If the boss loves night flights, he probably sleeps on the plane like a bear in hibernation. You, however, no matter how much you drink, read statistics or listen to Mozart, may spend the night squirming in your seat. Then by morning, when you're expected to be in top mental form for heavy negotiations, your speech may be sluggish and your concentration interrupted by visions of a Sealy Pos-turepedic.

You then fly back to the West Coast the same day to deliver a speech at the Rotary Club or attend little Joey's eighth-grade play. By 9 P.M., your body thinks it's midnight and you stagger home to get up early and return to work. The boss is back in the office (he slept on the flight home) so why shouldn't you be?

If you don't fare well on night flights, ask the boss if you can both take the last daytime flight east so you can get a night's sleep, pointing out that time saved on the "red-eye" will be lost in efficiency over the next few days. If you must take the red-eye, another strat-egy is to request compensating time off.

If you are required to fly on weekends or after work hours, are you working overtime? While some companies have regular policies of compensating time off to make up for such flights, others are fairly informal in this regard. Individuals who travel with the boss are often part of management and are expected, as one company president puts it, "not to act like an hourly employee."

The general practice, however, is for the boss to say "Thanks for the hard work. Why don't you take the morning off and sleep in?" The key to a good travel relationship is flexibility and consider-ation on both sides.

Working 10 Hours a Day

You need to be flexible too when business travel turns into 10- or 12-hour work days. "There's only so much time to get the most out of a business trip," says the president of a real estate research firm. "I expect my associates to put in whatever time it takes, not only to get the job done but to maximize the information-gathering opportunity. If that means a 10-hour day, so be it."

Not all traveling executives, however, enjoy the same health or stamina, and a boss should be cognizant that other bodies and minds may not function well on his timetable.

A young executive in excellent physical health but used to retiring by 10 P.M. often traveled with an older boss who was trying to lose weight. The boss, pepped up by diet pills, couldn't understand why his associate was averse to working into the night to finish paperwork. Although disinclined to admit he had trouble keeping up with the boss, the younger man finally decided it was better to say so than let his boss conclude he was lazy.

DINING WITH THE BOSS

When You Can't Say No

A partner in a law firm took a new assistant to Philadelphia for a meeting on a case. They arrived at dinner time. "A friend gave me some restaurant suggestions for this evening," he told the young man.

"Sorry, I made a dinner date with an old girlfriend here. I hope you don't mind dining without me?"

"No, go ahead," the boss said.

But he did mind. He hated eating alone and, on his next trip, he took a different assistant—a married one who wouldn't be looking up old flames.

What is the proper etiquette on a business trip? Do you leave the boss or employee alone if there's something better to do? After all, business hours are over. Don't your obligations end there?

Business travelers I've worked with, whether boss or employee, tend to agree that business travel may require obligations outside the normal business day. Yes, you are still working, but responsibilities to the people you travel with don't end at 5:30 or 6 P.M.

A vice president with girlfriends in various cities makes arrangements to meet his dates in the lounge of his hotel after dinner and invites the boss to join them for a drink, knowing the boss will decline and retire for the evening. Likewise, the president of an investment firm says that, if he has relatives or friends in a town he's visiting on business, he asks his associate to join them for dinner and never makes the employee feel like the "odd man out," particularly in an unfamiliar city, unless the associate seems to prefer it that way.

You shouldn't expect to bow out of dinner just because the boss has also invited a client or other business contact along. Just as you might feel insulted if the client invited the boss to dinner and ignored you, your company's guest might feel he or she wasn't important enough for your attention.

So when you're in New York, no matter how much you want to see a Broadway play or the Yankees versus the Dodgers or Aunt Betsy, your first commitment is to the job, even after hours. Of course, you can always suggest to the boss that inviting a potential client to the theater or sports activity might be the perfect way to break the ice and build rapport in a relaxed atmosphere.

When You're on a Diet

When you're on a diet and traveling alone, it's easy to stop at a market for an apple and diet soda and call it dinner. You wouldn't feel out of place either, seated at the counter of the hotel's coffee shop savoring the soup of the day and little else.

When traveling with the boss, however, be sure to advise her in advance if you're on any kind of diet. Otherwise, she may be embarrassed when she's pulled all strings for a reservation at the best restaurant in town and you order only a shrimp cocktail (or worse, you flourish a packet of vitamin powder for the chef to whip up). It's not good form to bring your own dinner, unobtrusive as it is, to a classy restaurant. If the boss knows in advance that you'll be eating very little, she'll have the option of choosing a more casual restaurant where one dinner more or less won't be noticed.

She may not have this option, however, when hosting a company client for dinner. If you order only a club soda with a twist of lime, the guest may feel uncomfortable ordering the caviar appetizer, Caesar salad and rack of lamb topped off by a chocolate soufflé. To remove any uneasiness, you could always say, "I'm on a diet, but may I suggest the salmon-en-croute?" If you suggest the highest-priced entree, the guest won't worry about your budget, although he or she may still feel gluttonous and pass on the soufflé. When the goal is to create a relaxed atmosphere for the guest, it might be better to order each course, take one bite and leave the rest. One manager I know, who has a problem resisting food once it's in front of him, will order something he can't bring himself to eat—snails, sweetbreads, tripe—or something like frog legs or pigeon. Since these entrees are so lean, no one notices when he simply rearranges the bones on his plate without taking a bite.

When the Boss Is on a Diet

A vice president of a real estate acquisition firm frequently travels with a boss who is always on a diet and a workaholic to boot. The boss doesn't eat breakfast, doesn't interrupt work to stop for lunch and dines around 8 P.M. when it's too dark to see real estate. The vice president is used to three square meals a day and doesn't feel energetic or insightful when his stomach commands attention with the subtlety of a drill sergeant. To solve the problem, he's invented reasons to stop at the local mini-market.

"I'll tell him I forgot to bring my toothbrush on the trip and when we stop at the 7-Eleven or Circle K, I run in and stuff my pockets with chocolate chip cookies or other junk food."

He also tries to arrange lunch appointments with potential buyers and sellers because the boss is willing to eat lunch if it means business.

If you're not in a position to arrange such meetings and your boss doesn't comprehend that your stomach growls to the beat of a different drummer, ask the hotel coffee shop to pack you a lunch.

WHO PAYS WHAT?

Companies have different ways to cover management and employee travel expenses. Some companies pay all expenses in advance or dole out company credit cards. Others reimburse travelers after they submit an account of expenses. Most use a combination of both methods, i.e., paying for airline tickets in advance but reimbursing hotel, meal, telephone and automobile expenses later. In some cases, it's much later.

Problems arise when a company traveler is expected to use a personal credit card to pay expenses that are out of his normal budget. Particularly when expense reports are submitted to an out-of-state headquarters, the reimbursement can take months. In the meantime, the traveler may have to cover a few thousand dollars of credit card expenses immediately or incur interest charges. These charges are compounded when traveling with a boss in an upgraded style—flying first class, staying at the Ritz Carlton instead of the Holiday Inn and dining at a five-star restaurant instead of McDonald's.

When the boss is also the owner of the company, he'll usually pick up the tab for everything since expenses will revert to him anyway. Larger corporations may require that expenses be reported separately because they are paid out of separate accounts or billed to separate projects.

If you have difficulty covering travel expenses until reimbursed, you should anticipate what extra funds you'll need to meet your credit card payment and ask the company for an advance against expenses.

Side Trips

Frequently, a business traveler will call the company's travel agent after reservations have already been ordered by the boss's secretary and say, "As long as I'm going to be in Washington, D.C., on business, I'd like to pop up to Pittsburgh and visit the folks over the weekend. Can I exchange this business-class ticket for a coach ticket that will include Pittsburgh at no extra cost?"

While most side trips can be worked out so any extra costs are charged to the traveler, there are a couple of pitfalls to watch for. The boss may expect to take advantage of the flight time to brief you or vice versa. If she's sitting in business class and you're in the coach section, you'll need walkie-talkies to communicate. She may also be insulted that you opted to sit apart. In other words, be sure you discuss any changes with the boss beforehand.

Even when you and your boss are seated together, if your ticket carries a different fare basis code, the two of you could still be split up. An auditor changed his full coach ticket to Boston to an excursion fare to include Hartford, Connecticut, at little extra cost. Although he told his boss about the extra stop, he neglected to tell him the new ticket was priced at a lower, more restrictive fare. They flew together as far as St. Louis, where the connection to Boston was canceled due to mechanical problems. The boss and other passengers holding full-fare tickets were accommodated on a flight with another carrier, while the auditor had to wait four hours for the next available seat on the same airline and missed the meeting in Boston. (He now sells used cars.)

In another case, a client and his boss reached their destination in Europe on time, but the client they planned to meet was delayed by weather. The boss had no problem extending his stay a day on his full-fare ticket, but the associate's ticket had been priced at a non-refundable excursion rate to include a personal deviation at the lowest cost. His ticket could not be extended without upgrading to a much higher fare. In the end, it cost the associate much more money than he had bargained for.

Be sure you are aware of the restrictions tagged to a lower fare. Ask your travel agent to spell them out on your itinerary or ticket if you tend to forget. Then think about "what ifs"—What if we're late, the meeting gets postponed, the meeting place is changed. After you've played out all these scenarios, you can decide if the restrictive fare is likely to cause more problems than it's worth.

Dining Out

Sometimes, you and your boss are allotted a per diem to cover meal expenses. If your allotments are the same, chances are you'll agree on a restaurant within your budgets. If the boss's per diem is higher, his choice of restaurant may be out of your range. Or if his salary is significantly higher, he may not mind paying out of pocket to dine in style. If you do mind, point out the difference in per diem and let the boss offer to treat you.

It's more likely that the boss will pick up the associate's tab for meals on the road. Both can feel awkward, however, when the waiter presents the check to the male vice president, who then hands it over to his female boss.

One man, an assistant to a female writer, travels with his boss around the country on lecture and talk-show tours. It doesn't bother him to turn over the check to a woman. Another vice president, however, "felt like a gigolo" when the president, an older woman, took the check in public places. They solved the problem with a corporate credit card in his name, which he carries and uses to charge all travel expenses. The credit card charges are paid eventually by the company's controller. Another female boss and her male secretary usually dine and entertain at their hotel. That way, meals and drinks are signed to the room and then paid at check-out on the boss's credit card.

Should you treat the boss occasionally? Some bosses consider it a compliment to their management style if an employee buys them lunch or a drink once in awhile. They enjoy the feeling of camaraderie or appreciation expressed. Other bosses prefer not to be treated on a trip. "The tab will just come back to me, buried in an expense report," says one company manager.

When a client is along as a guest of the firm, your attempt to pick up the check, regardless of good intentions, could be perceived as a move to undermine the authority of the boss.

The head of an advertising agency flew to Denver to pitch an idea to a potential client. She took along the account executive who would be working with the client. She was surprised when the junior man paid the tab for the threesome at dinner, something he had never done before. She was more surprised when the bill appeared for reimbursement on the man's expense account. It all made sense, however, when she discovered he was resigning from her firm to set up his own shop and wanted to impress her clients so he could take their business with him. Now she leaves the account executives home when meeting a client.

SEXUAL HARASSMENT

Kathy, a beautiful young actress, recalls a trip she took with her one-time boss, the head of a marketing company. When she interviewed for a job with his firm, she explained frankly that she possessed no prior office experience. She was surprised when he hired her anyway as his assistant, and she took the job because she needed money to pay the rent between infrequent acting jobs. A short time later the boss asked her to accompany him to New York on a business trip.

"Since the boss told me his girlfriend was going on the trip too, I didn't anticipate any problems in the male-female department and didn't question my role on the trip."

At the airport, she learned that the "girlfriend" couldn't make it. At the hotel, the boss checked them into a one-bedroom, two-bath suite, explaining that he expected her to work closely with him so she could take charge of the client's new promotion campaign. When he ordered wine and dinner from room service instead of going out to a restaurant, she began to understand what kind of "work" he had in mind. She spent the evening side-stepping his physical advances. "I wanted to tell him off, but I had twenty-five dollars in my wallet and he had my ticket home. He finally gave up on me and retired to the bedroom. I locked the door of the second bathroom and spent an uncomfortable night trying to sleep with a pillow and blanket in the bathtub. He sent me home the next day. I slept like a baby all the way to Los Angeles and never went back to work."

For Kathy, quitting her "side" job was not a difficult choice. However, for people who like their jobs and the company they work for, quitting or suing a boss for sexual harassment is not a favored solution. What can you do when traveling with a boss who makes you uncomfortable with his or her advances? While a businesslike manner or a few frank words of discouragement are usually enough to set the record straight, here are a few steps to follow when your words are ignored. That way, you'll never have to sleep in the bathtub.

1. If you anticipate problems, ask to make your own hotel and airline reservations. That way, you'll be sure of the room arrangements in advance.

2. Carry your own tickets for airlines, rail or other transportation.

3. Carry your own passport and visas if traveling outside the United States.

4. Carry your own room key.

5. Carry a major credit card with enough credit to get you home from your farthest point and enough cash for a few days on your own, if necessary.

6. When traveling to an unfamiliar city, carry your own map and telephone guide to services like taxicabs, airlines, embassies, police.

7. If unfamiliar with the language, carry a small translation dictionary.

On the other hand, many a fine romance has sprung from traveling with the boss. The assistant buyer for a large department store chain logged a mere 10,000 miles with the boss before they married and lived happily ever after.

While sexual harassment is a serious subject, I do know a few stories with happy endings—and they all started with travel.

DO'S AND DON'TS

Finally, here are some do's and don'ts when traveling with the boss.

Don't Be Late

Promptness is a virtue worth cultivating for every circumstance, but it's critical for business travel.

You have no control over the tardiness of airlines, baggage arrivals, transfer services, hotel-room readiness or traffic. Your promptness is the one factor you can control and one your boss will appreciate, particularly if he's already nervous about the trip. Don't leave him pacing at the gate wondering if you're going to miss the flight.

Don't Check Baggage

Most business trips last a few days to a week at most. Unless you're carrying special equipment, you can usually get by with a bag that fits under the seat in front of you and/or a garment bag that can be hung in the cabin. One consultant balked when her boss insisted she use carry-on luggage like he did. He wasn't going to wait for anyone to retrieve luggage from the carousel. However, after a few trips, she began to like the idea of not waiting the half-hour to hour in baggage claim or filing lost luggage reports. Now, even when she travels on a two-week vacation, she manages with carry-on bags only. "If all my clothes aren't dirty when I come home, I know I haven't packed efficiently," she says.

Keep in mind too that on smaller, nonjet aircraft, where there's little in-cabin space, your usual carry-on bag may not fit under the seat or in an overhead bin and may have to be checked as baggage. Check your itinerary for the type of aircraft (e.g., 737, 747), particularly as many small commuter airlines carry the name designation of a larger carrier in airline computer systems. United Airline flights between Los Angeles and San Francisco, for example, are usually 737 passenger jets. United Express flights between Los Angeles and Fresno, on the other hand, are usually smaller Jetstream 31 turbo-props with 18 or 19 seats.

Dress Appropriately

Jeans and a tee shirt may be your idea of comfortable dress for travel, but if your boss is dressed in a three-piece suit, he or she may feel uncomfortable with the image you are projecting for the company. If in doubt, ask what activities and attire will be required of you. Or, take your cue from the way the chief dresses—unless of course, the boss shows up for a $2 million loan meeting with a bank president in a tank top and tennies.

Don't Gossip

A quick way to torpedo your rapport with the boss is by launching misguided missiles of office gossip. It's a good way to put the boss on notice that whatever he tells you in confidence will likely end up as office gossip as well.

Don't Ask for a Raise on the Road

Just because the boss is cornered in the window seat of a 747 doesn't make it the right time to ask for a raise. If the chief is not prepared for a salary review, he or she may give you the wrong answer or evade the question altogether, casting a pall over the rest of the trip. Next time, the boss might leave you at home rather than give you another opportunity to hit him up for a raise. Pick a more appropriate time to discuss the subject when you're back home.

Don't Be a Prima Donna

"I'm not getting up for a 7 A.M. flight." "Have the front desk change my room. It's so small, I'm getting claustrophobia." "You don't want to eat at that restaurant chain do you? Their food is lousy." "I need a limousine pickup. I can't stand unkempt taxis."

Such talk may get you accommodated the way you would like, but it can also earn you the reputation of royal pain in the neck.

Particularly when traveling with more than one colleague, the boss has enough to do without catering to everyone's personal whims. Fitting into the common denominator and the expense account is part of the art of traveling with the boss.

FIVE

How to Survive Traveling with Friends

Advantages

Marty dropped off his wife, Joanne, at the Chicago airport three hours ahead of her domestic flight. She was meeting a girlfriend she hadn't seen since college. Together, they were flying to a college reunion in San Francisco.

Three hours later, Marty got a phone call from his wife. "Can you come and get us? We missed the plane."

Already comfortable in his pajamas, Marty was incredulous. "How could you miss the plane? You were there three hours early!"

"Well," Joanne answered, "Stephanie and I had so much to catch up on, we went to get a cup of coffee. We started talking and lost track of time. When we finally realized it, we ran to the gate but the plane was already taxiing down the runway. There's no more flights until morning. Can you come get us?"

"Gee, honey, it's the last quarter of the football game. Why don't you stay at an airport hotel and you and Stephanie can talk until morning?"

Any other time, Joanne would have been slightly miffed by

his attitude, but she enjoyed Stephanie's company and thought it was a great idea. "Thanks, darling," she told him. "It's really sweet of you to treat us for the night. I'll just put it on your credit card."

Which brings us to the main reason friends travel together—they enjoy each other's company. But there are other advantages to traveling with friends.

A number of my clients routinely take their vacations with friends. When I asked two couples why they traveled with each other year after year, each member cited a different advantage.

Phil was the designated organizer for the group. As a broker, he had time after the stock market closed to work out the details with the travel agent. For him, the main advantages were economical. "We save money on car rentals, particularly in Europe where rental taxes and gasoline costs are high." Where possible, they shared a condominium with a kitchen and saved on some meal expenses. The wives confirmed they didn't mind cooking on vacation when they could chat with each other and share the work. Since they all enjoyed bridge, they saved money on outside entertainment by staying in some evenings to play cards.

Phil's wife, Marie, felt the big advantage was their collective language power. While each marriage partner spoke only one second language, together they covered English, Spanish, French, German and Italian, enough to bargain their way through the world's major flea markets.

Her friend Nicole enjoyed the trips for the shared activities and conversation, particularly since Phil arranged everything and she didn't have to plan a thing.

Nicole's husband, John, was grateful that Phil and Marie were along to share the driving. Nicole didn't drive the manual automobiles that were most economical and prevalent in Europe. With his friends, he could relax at times and enjoy the scenery.

They all agreed, however, that when they traveled with friends, the trip wasn't over when it was over. The stories and shared memories would keep them laughing for years to come.

Disadvantages

If you like your friends, why not travel together? The more the merrier, right? "Wrong," says Joanne, who traveled with another couple and vowed never to do it again.

"First of all, we had no privacy. Sometimes my husband had business calls from the office, and since the only telephone was in the living room of the suite, our friends learned all our business. Even when we didn't share a suite, our rooms were adjacent and my husband and I felt we had to watch every word.

"I also felt I had to be sociable whether or not I was in the mood. Sometimes when I just wanted to retreat to my room and read, I felt compelled to make small talk instead.

"Besides, it cost us more than if we'd gone alone. For some reason, every time it was our turn to pick up the check, we were at a 'better' restaurant. Since we shared suites, hotel costs were higher too.

"Worse, we didn't get to see half of the sights we were interested in because our friends were never on time. That caused a lot of tension, and in the end, I think it ruined our friendship too."

The lesson of this unhappy experience is that *good friends don't always make good travel companions.* Some people travel with friends to get to know each other better. But there are certain things you should know about each other before you ever share a closet.

Are You Compatible Travel Types?

How can you determine in advance which friends or acquaintances are likely to make compatible travel companions?

Having read the Introduction, you probably already know

whether you're a comfort seeker, adventurer, beach bum or other travel type. Or you may be some combination of two or more types.

What about the friends you want to travel with? Don't assume that just because you share a love of sushi, you have enough in common to travel successfully together through Japan. If you haven't discussed travel preferences with potential companions, you can start by asking them where they've been before. That's what travel agents do before making trip recommendations.

When a client tells me he wants to go somewhere he can windsurf, I'll ask, "Where have you been already and how did you like it?" If he answers, "The Four Seasons in Maui and I loved it," then I know the client is probably a beach bum who also likes a high degree of comfort. (The Four Seasons is a deluxe hotel in the Hawaiian islands.) He might be a relaxer too. To find out, I would ask him what else he did while he was there. If he says, "Nothing. It was great," I would probably recommend a deluxe resort that offers windsurfing and is "away from it all."

If, however, he tells me he rented a car and toured the island for a couple days, discoed in town and visited a museum, I would look instead for a deluxe resort with windsurfing located in or close to a town that offered art galleries and nightlife as well.

You can use the same technique to obtain clues to your friends' travel types. The more friends along, the tougher compatibility becomes. When two couples travel together, for example, there may be four different types or combinations to satisfy.

Once you determine travel types, you can seek a destination compatible to all. But before you choose *where* to go, you need to answer the following questions.

Are Your Budgets Compatible?

A colleague told me about her Uncle Joe, who was a postal

clerk in Little Rock, Arkansas. Each year, he and his wife spent their vacation visiting her mother in Wichita, Kansas, but he longed to see more of the United States. He and a coworker decided that they and their wives would rent a recreational vehicle (RV) on their next vacation and drive together through the national parks of Utah and Wyoming for a week. The coworker would then return the vehicle to Little Rock while Joe and his wife made their yearly visit to her relatives.

Since both postal workers earned the same salary, brown-bagged their lunches and drove the same model Ford, Joe assumed their budgets for the trip would be the same. When he returned unused tickets to Wichita to his travel agent niece for a refund, she was surprised.

"I'll never do that again," her uncle explained. "We spent all the money I budgeted for our vacation so we came home instead of going to Wichita. I thought we would save money by cooking and sleeping in the RV. But my buddy kept buying strawberries and filet mignon. Our half of the grocery bill was more than we would've spent in restaurants. They insisted on sleeping every couple of days in a motel so they could have a large bed and tub." According to his niece, Joe is still trying to explain the no-show to his mother-in-law.

It doesn't necessarily follow that friends in the same tax bracket will have saved or budgeted the same amount for a trip. One way to set the record straight is to ask your friends, "What do you think it'll cost me for this portion of the trip?" Or simply tell them that you want to keep your trip costs under $500, $5,000 or whatever figure you choose. That way your friends will either be considerate of your budget or you probably won't be traveling with them again.

On the other hand, some travelers may find their friends' frugality embarrassing.

I traveled with a college friend one summer before attending classes at Cambridge, England. With a copy of Arthur Frommer's

Europe on $5 a Day tucked under my arm, I was prepared to stretch my scholarship dollars to last through school. My friend Lynn was frugal too, but with a flair. When we purchased passage on the overnight ferry from Dublin to Glasgow, neither one of us wanted to spend the extra money for a cabin. When some younger crew members asked why we didn't have a cabin, Lynn announced that we were writing a book called *Europe on $2 a Day.*

Word quickly spread and the crew went out of their way to help us with the "book." We were introduced to the captain, who gave us a tour of the bridge and invited us to his cabin for a glass of sherry. After Lynn filled him in on the "book," he summoned an officer to show us to a private cabin "on the house."

I was embarrassed to be the recipient of favors under false pretenses. "Lynn," I whispered, "how could you tell that big fib about *Europe on $2 a Day?*

"It worked, didn't it?" she replied. "And who knows, we *might* write a book."

Well, that was different. I felt better. Besides, as we soon discovered, it wasn't just our "book" the crew was interested in. When the officer tried to follow us into the cabin, Lynn hit him with her umbrella to keep him out. Neither one of us had bargained for him as part of our $2-a-day experience.

Not all travelers are willing to go to the same lengths, however, for the sake of economy. A college student, Diana, had just received her teaching credential when she set out with another new teacher on a trip through the Pacific Northwest. It was a Saturday night toward the end of their drive when they pulled into a town amid the wheat fields of Idaho. Rough-looking cowhands with straw sticking out from between their teeth loitered about. The girls stopped a potbellied officer who turned out to be the local sheriff.

"Where's a good place to camp out?" Diana's friend asked.

"This is no place for two young girls to camp out," the sheriff responded, recommending a motel down the road.

"But we only have $35 left and we need that for gas to get us home," the friend insisted.

Diana wanted to sink into the seat and disappear. The story wasn't true. They didn't have a lot of money, but they had enough for a motel.

Feeling sorry for them, the sheriff took them home where his wife fed them dinner, put them up overnight and provided breakfast the following morning. Diana didn't like representing herself as a charity case when she wasn't. She was so embarrassed she never traveled with that friend again.

Are Your Personalities and Habits Compatible?

People can have personalities as different as Popeye and Captain Bligh and yet be friends. When friends get together a few hours a week, these differences can be stimulating and endearing. But some personality traits we find attractive or tolerable in the short term may become more pronounced and frustrating when friends are together for longer periods.

A teacher friend named Jill toured Russia with another teacher, Alicia, who taught at the same school and spoke a little Russian. They were travel enthusiasts who preferred to travel independently of any group. Jill soon discovered that her friend was too "romantically adventuresome." Alicia, it seems, fell in love with a different Russian in every city they visited. "Every evening she would go out somewhere with a local fellow and I would be left by myself," Jill recalls.

"One night in Odessa, she didn't come back at all. She knew our flight left at noon, so I figured something must have happened to her, but I had no idea where to find her. Frantic, I alerted the

American Embassy that she was missing. They took my report and I was told to call if I heard anything."

At 10:30 A.M., Alicia breezed through the door, explaining she'd spent the night with a pilot in the Russian air force. He even took her to his training base and left her standing inside the gate, with camera bag and telephoto lens, while he obtained permission for leave. Alicia was aglow from the adventure.

"Are you crazy?" Jill asked. "I didn't know if you had been arrested or kidnapped and shipped to Siberia!"

Travel often brings out a habit or personality trait that may have gone unnoticed even if two people have been friends a dozen years. Sometimes, only after they've traveled together can they know if they would do it again.

"I would still travel with Alicia to places where I could manage alone," says Jill. "She's a fun person when she's around, but she's not as careful as I like to be. I don't think I'll go with her to the valley of the headhunters in New Guinea."

Even when you and your friends have compatible personalities, certain habits can drive you crazy. If you're a nonsmoker, you may tolerate the smoking habit of friends when you entertain each other. But the habit may become irritating when you share the same car, hotel room or other space all day.

DECISIONS TO SHARE UP FRONT

One Person to Handle Arrangements

Once in awhile I get a call from a client that fills me with dread. It goes something like this: "My wife and I will be traveling with three other couples from our horticulture club to the Tulip

Show in Holland. Please book Skylark Airlines and the Wooden Shoe Hotel for all of us. The others will be calling you for details."

Two days later, the second couple calls. "Let's not go on Skylark Airlines. The last time, instead of the fruit platter we ordered, we got the children's hamburger special with Snoopy cookies."

The third couple asks me to switch the party to the Windmill Hotel because their Uncle Benny stayed there 40 years ago and loved it. The fourth couple never surfaces. When they are finally tracked down for payment, they exclaim, "Oh, we got tickets from my niece. She's a travel agent too. Didn't anyone tell you? Of course we want to sit next to our friends on the plane and we want our hotel rooms to be adjacent."

Having your friends call separately about the same trip may be a good way to drive your travel agent crazy, but it doesn't make for the most harmonious trip. An orchestra of fine soloists still needs a conductor to set the pace and keep notes from bumping into each other. Likewise, friends who travel together need one person to coordinate plans. The more people traveling together, the more important it becomes to let one member of the party coordinate with the airline, hotel or travel agent.

A group of five friends was traveling together to Puerta Vallarta at New Year's, a time when airline and hotel space is sold out well in advance. One of the five made the initial arrangements but the others called the airlines later with deviations. When one member of the group called the airline to cancel his reservation completely, he didn't realize that his friend Dick was on the same passenger name record. The airline reservationist asked if he was making a complete cancellation. He answered yes, thinking she meant "round trip." Dick's reservation was canceled too and he could not get another until two days later. As a result Dick wasted one night of a prepaid hotel package, and a sheepish friend is still in the doghouse.

An acquaintance and her husband who travel with five other couples each ski season avoid such chaos by rotating leadership. Each year someone else in the party chooses the destination, hotel and airline schedule and handles all the arrangements with the travel agent. They travel the same week every year, so everyone knows to set that week aside. If anyone in the party needs to modify plans to accommodate personal problems, they do so through the designated planner. That limits opportunities for mix-ups on reservations and deposits.

Because this group has been traveling together successfully for 23 years, each friend knows who prefers twin beds, who must have a private bathroom and who can't get up before 8 A.M. For friends traveling together for the first time, here are some other decisions to discuss before the designated coordinator goes ahead with reservations.

When, Where and How Long?

Deciding you want to go to Rio de Janeiro for Christmas is not enough. Before your coordinator can make arrangements, you need to decide as a group the dates you'll depart and return. Your coordinator needs to know each person's flexibility too, so he can make decisions when flight, hotel or tour availabilities don't quite match your chosen dates. That means knowing that Pepe has to be back at work by January 5 and Olga can't leave until after her exam on December 20.

The *where* and *how long* part may sound easy—Rio for two weeks. But is two weeks too long in one city? Is there time for Iguassú Falls, Manaus or Buenos Aires? Are these places worthwhile or does visiting them entail too much running around and too much expense? Until research begins or a travel agent makes recommendations, you may not be able to make these decisions or even be aware of the options. But as a group, whether four or fourteen, you could decide on the minimum days you want to spend in Rio and the time left for other places. Then the coordinator can come back to the group with a suggested itinerary and projected expense for approval before finalizing reservations.

Accommodations

Some friends may have a specific hotel or resort in mind for their trip. Sometimes, however, you may have no familiarity with accommodations at your destination or what the rates are likely to be at each. While you can't pick specific lodgings at this point, you can decide whether you will share rooms or need separate accommodations; whether you prefer budget, moderate or deluxe hotels; the maximum you wish to spend per night; and whether you prefer hotels or condominiums.

When friends decide to share a suite or condo, there are additional decisions to make. Who will get the bedroom with the king-size bed? The bedroom with the television, the fireplace or the lake view? You might decide to alternate or flip a coin for these amenities so no one feels short-changed on the trip.

Dining

Two couples who played tennis and golf together at the same country club in Montana decided to escape winter together at a resort in Scottsdale, Arizona. They had much in common until it was time for dinner. One of the husbands, Jim, had started a Pritikin program and wanted to avoid foods with butter, oil, sugars and fats. That eliminated Italian and French restaurants and steak houses. His wife, Stephanie, was allergic to wheat and MSG. That eliminated breads, noodles, cakes and Chinese foods. The other wife hated fish and, because of a chronic intestinal problem, couldn't digest lettuce and other gas-producing foods. Her husband, Joe, was a meat-and-potatoes man who hated vegetables. His idea of a vacation included generous cuts of rare prime rib.

The "Where shall we go for dinner?" discussion would begin about 5 P.M. and continue into the evening as each person's restaurant suggestions were shot down by someone else's respective dietary problem. Finally, to compromise, they ended up at a restaurant where no one was happy.

For some, dining is nothing more than an essential interruption of more interesting activities. When, where and what they eat is inconsequential and plays no part in their vacation planning. For others, however, dining is entertainment and a memorable part of the travel experience. These are the travelers who solicit restaurant suggestions from friends before they depart and take delight afterward in describing the texture of the sauce on the veal Florentine at a countryside restaurant in Tuscany.

While most friends have dined together prior to traveling together, they often put aside their dietary habits for an occasional night out at a restaurant. On vacation, however, when dining out several evenings in succession, they may be less willing or less able to slough over dietary restrictions.

If you're the sort who can compromise easily without feeling deprived, your friends' special requirements won't matter. If not, be sure to discuss food preferences in advance. Otherwise, you may find your friends' choices in cuisine too tough to swallow.

Friends whose eating habits differ can simplify this problem by agreeing to go their separate ways at dinner time. Another alternative is to stay in condos or suites with kitchens where you can each cook your favorite foods and still share each other's company over dinner.

Think too about *when* you'll eat. This is particularly important when on the move—driving from point to point on a given schedule.

Two friends were driving through Europe hoping to see as much as possible in two weeks. After sightseeing in each town, one liked to be on the road quickly to the next point of interest. His friend, however, was a constant snacker. In addition to breakfast, lunch and dinner he insisted on stopping for a bite at every bakery and fast-food outlet along the way. His friend gave up trying to hurry his pal with the voracious appetite. Instead, he used the time his friend spent in line at the Bavarian sausage stand to gas up the car or buy maps and other essentials. That way, he didn't feel they were wasting time.

A teacher used to dining at 6:00 P.M. each day adjusted to dinner at 8 P.M. by eating lunch later or snacking in the late afternoon. A couple accustomed to dining late adjusted to the early dinner seating on a cruise ship to accommodate a diabetic friend's schedule. Then they were ready to "pig out" again at the midnight buffet.

If you can make such adjustments without resenting them, then, as they say in Swahili, *hakuna matata,* "no problem." Once you agree to travel with friends, you have, in fact, agreed to keep your mouth from echoing any grumbling in your stomach.

You'll also want to decide collectively whether you'll dine out, dine in on take-out, cook in the condo or some combination thereof. Be sure that if you split the bills or alternate picking up the tab, the meals or restaurants you choose are somewhat commensurate. If, for example, your friend pays the tab at the five-star French restaurant, don't figure you're off the hook the next night with a bucket of fried chicken.

You don't have to dine like Henry VIII every night, but if your turn to pay comes at a much cheaper restaurant, offer to pick up the tab for entertainment or some other expense too. On the other hand, if you don't think your friends are picking up their fair share, suggest you all pay your own tabs separately. Although you may not mind treating your companions in order to dine your way, remember that few people want to feel they owe you. Allow your friends to pay their share even if it means dining in a less expensive style. Otherwise, they may feel uncomfortable traveling with you. Naturally, there are exceptions, as when they agree to be your guest for a "big splurge" celebrating your roulette winnings.

Shared Activities

The same principle of contributing commensurate costs applies to entertainment, sightseeing, transportation and other non-personal expenses. But you should also have an understanding of how much time you're expected to commit to shared activities.

Two couples from opposite coasts of the United States met by chance in the Caribbean one winter. They discovered they had much in common: they originally hailed from the same town where they shared acquaintances, their teenagers attended the same college in Denver, and the husbands' companies did business with each other—a fact that kept them in contact later. The following year, the couples agreed to vacation together at the same resort on another Caribbean island, where they soon realized "together" held different implications for each couple.

The Waldons figured they would get together for dinner with their new friends and "see them around." The Dunfeys, however, expected to do everything together including sightseeing, shopping, golf and casino hopping. The Waldons, who enjoyed time to themselves, were not prepared psychologically for companions tagging along as they shopped or explored the nooks and crannies of the town. They began to look for ways to escape. One evening they excused themselves from the following day's activities, explaining that acquaintances who lived on the island had invited them to go sailing on their yacht.

Actually, there had been no such invitation. The Waldons sneaked away to a secluded beach to windsurf by themselves. After they put out past the waves, they looked back and were appalled to see the Dunfeys had chosen the same secluded beach and were lying down within yards of their own blanket. Afraid to be discovered, the Waldons stayed out several hours on the water, until the other couple left, before reclaiming their gear on the beach. The Waldons then had a legitimate reason to excuse themselves from dinner. They were too sunburned to move.

Misunderstandings can be avoided if you're clear about your time when making plans. If you want to limit your time commitment, you can tell your friends, for example, that you already have plans in London on Tuesday and Wednesday but would love company on your side trip to Bath. Or, "I have a lot of reading to catch up on, but I'd love to play a few rounds of golf with you." This way your friends will have an opportunity to plan some activities on their own too and won't feel slighted.

Who Drives?

If you and your friends select a vacation that involves driving, here are some points to consider:

1. Which car will seat the group most comfortably?
2. Which trunk will best accommodate the groups' luggage? Be sure to limit each person's luggage allotment to the sizes that will fit.
3. Is the car in good enough shape to withstand the proposed wear and tear?
4. Is the car prepared for emergencies? It should carry a good

spare tire, jack, chains if headed for snow, first-aid kit, flash-light and flares.

5. Who will alternate driving? This could be important if the car has a manual transmission that only the owner can drive.

6. What are the house rules for your car (such as no smoking or no munching on watermelon or sunflower seeds)?

7. How will you handle expenses for gas, oil, tolls and parking? Will you split as you go, alternate or keep an expense log to split costs at the end? Who gets the receipts for the IRS if the trip is deductible?

8. Who pays for breakdowns, damage or traffic violations?

The last point might seem obvious. Since the driver is in con-trol, isn't he responsible? Not necessarily. One teenager was driving his friend's car on a trip they took to the mountains when they were hit by an uninsured motorist. The friend who owned the car carried insurance that would cover the damage costs less a $300 deductible. He felt his friend should at least split the cost of the deductible since he was driving. The latter, however, felt the owner should pay every-thing, as the accident was someone else's fault and, if it were his car, he would pay.

"But you don't have a car," the owner countered.

"True," the driver replied, "but if I had one, I would pay the deductible."

In the end, the owner's father paid the deductible.

Legally, if the car owner allows someone else to drive the car, he assumes responsibility for that driver. If you don't want to risk damage to your car but prefer to share the driving tasks, you can leave your own car at home and rent one with full insurance cover-age, provided you're over 21. (Some rental agencies have a minimum rental age of 25 or charge more if you're 21 to 25.)

While the driver is responsible for moving violations, the car owner or renter is ultimately responsible for parking tickets. So if your travel companions make a collective decision to ignore a No Parking sign, be sure they understand they're expected to contribute to potential fines.

I was in Carmel, California, once with three friends when we agreed to park in a white zone and split the cost of the inevitable $15 ticket. Having searched 30 minutes for a legitimate parking spot, we were convinced it was the only alternative within a mile of town. Our feet seconded the motion. We returned four hours later expecting to be out $3.75 each. To our chagrin, there were not one, but four parking tickets on the windshield. We learned another lesson of the road—don't park illegally in a small town where parking fines are likely to be a major source of public revenue.

PITFALLS

I'll Let You Know If We Can Come

"We're going to Africa on a safari in December," you tell your friends.

"We would love to do that. Can we join you?" they ask in a burst of enthusiasm.

"Great," you reply. "I'll make all the arrangements." And you do, reserving another room and a private guide with a van large enough for all of you. You cost it out and ask your friends for their share of the payment.

"Well, my mother isn't feeling well and we're trying to sell our house . . . er . . . can I let you know?"

Now what do you do? If you make the deposits, you might get stuck with penalties. If you don't, you could lose your reservations. And of course, the arrangements will cost more if you now have to bear some expenses, such as the van and guide, alone. If you're organizing a trip that involves friends, be sure you give them three deadline dates.

1. Last day to let you know if they're coming.

2. Last day to pay.

3. Last day to cancel without penalties.

When friends agree to join you on a trip, send them a copy of the itinerary with the deposit due date as soon as possible. A request for money is like a cold shower after an all-night party and tends to have a sobering effect on plans that weren't completely thought out.

Altering Plans to Accommodate Others

The Thompsons were a comfort-seeking couple who always booked well in advance to obtain the best hotel and most convenient flights. One year, however, they called a few weeks before their departure to "downgrade." Friends would be joining them who could not afford deluxe arrangements. We changed their hotel to tourist class and their business-class air reservations to coach so they could sit together. The dates of travel were changed too because the other husband had to be home for an escrow closing. A few days before departure, the Thompsons called again.

"Remember those 9 flights and 12 hotels you changed for us? Could you change them back to our original reservations? Our friends can't go with us now."

Unfortunately, at the height of the season, the deluxe hotels were sold out as were business-class seats on the plane, so the Thompsons set out on a trip that was perfect for their friends but not for them.

When you alter your plans to suit someone else, ask yourself,

"Will I still be happy if they cancel?" If the answer is no, don't do it, no matter how much you like your friends. If the answer is "I really don't care," you'll probably enjoy your friends' trip plans anyway. But once you have made the decision, don't blame your friends for the trip you never wanted. After all, you agreed to make the adjustments.

Changes and Deviations

The more people you travel with, the more apt you are to have requests for changes and deviations. Even when plans are made well in advance, it's often not until the week before departure that friends fully focus on their trip and notice the time conflicts with their high-school reunion picnic or that while in Chicago, they will be a short distance from their nephew in Madison, Wisconsin, and now want to return home from there. Unexpected obstacles such as a sick child, a broken leg or your name called as a game-show contestant can crop up at the last minute.

The question, then, is how to handle changes or deviations efficiently, because the more changes, the greater the possibilities for error.

The first favor you can do yourself is to read the itinerary thoroughly when you receive it. Don't wait until you're in a cab to Kennedy Airport before noticing the flight leaves from Newark. Second, try to keep any changes or deviations to a minimum. Third, when making changes, be sure to repeat any special requests. When one couple agreed to join friends on a trip to New Orleans, they requested a hotel room with a window that could be opened and closed because the wife had claustrophobia. Five months later, when they changed the dates of their stay, they didn't reiterate the open-window request—they expected their group leader to remember it.

He didn't, and the couple had to change rooms three times to stay in available rooms with windows.

Don't bet that your coordinator or travel agent is going to remember every little request you made several months ago. Today, many computerized travel agencies don't use paper at all; special requests are noted on your reservation record in the computer. If that record is canceled and new reservations are made, the original notes are gone from view.

Fourth, be sure that any arrangements affected by your changes are reconfirmed or changed as well. A couple won a trip to Hawaii as part of the husband's top-selling performance for his company. Several dinners were also arranged for them and the other "top producers." When the couple called to delay their arrival date at the hotel by one day, the coordinator canceled them off the evening dinner as well. He saw no reason to tell them that the luau-themed dinner they would be missing had been changed to a business-attire event. The couple, however, was merely staying with relatives their first night in Hawaii and showed up for dinner at the hotel decked out in grass skirts, straw hats and ukuleles.

Odd Man Out

Upon graduation from high school, Joanne joined a friend, Anita, and another girl on a trip through Europe. It turned out, however, that the other two girls were closer friends with similar personalities. Whenever a decision was to be made on where to go or what to do, Joanne was overruled by the other two girls. Her parents sensed her growing isolation with each letter home. From Paris, she wrote that Anita and Trudy had gone shopping while she had gone alone to Notre Dame and the Bastille. Since it was after eight o'clock and they had not returned, she was skipping dinner and going to bed early.

Concerned that she was homesick and not having a good time, her parents discussed flying to Europe to join her. A few days later, they received another letter from Florence, Italy.

"Anita and Trudy went shopping so I went to the Uffizi Art Museum by myself and met this darling boy, Mario. He took me all around Florence on the back of his motorcycle. It was great. Tonight I'm going out with Mario and his friends Georgio, Bruno, Luciano and Roberto. Can't wait. Love, Joanne."

Now her parents were worried she was having too good a time. They caught up with her by telephone in Perugia. Anita and Trudy had gone shopping, and Joanne and Mario were just leaving for an Etruscan art exhibit.

"Darling, do you want to come home or would you like us to meet you in Rome?" her parents asked.

"Well, I'll be staying with Mario's folks in Rome and I don't think they have any more room. They said I could stay as long as I want."

Now her parents worried that she might never come home.

Fortunately, when Joanne realized the other girls weren't willing to accommodate her in their itinerary, she was independent enough to make her own good time. A traveler who is less self-reliant, however, may not adapt as well when feeling left out. Two people traveling together tend to compromise because they want each other's company. Larger groups of travelers tend to break into smaller cliques, providing some options for every personality. Before you join a group of two or four, you may want to ask yourself how well you'll fit in and, if there's a chance that you won't, how well you will manage as the "odd man out."

Trust Me

Two friends set out on a camping trip to Glacier National Park between Montana and Alberta, Canada. Bill had never been camping and let his friend, Eugene, make most of the decisions.

Eugene insisted on leaving their food supplies on a picnic table overnight at the campsite. When Bill suggested they would be safer left in the car, Eugene insisted, "We always put the supplies out so they'll be ready in the morning."

When they crawled into their sleeping bags, Bill still felt uneasy, particularly since everyone else in the camp was sleeping in trailers or vans.

The boys were awakened in the night by cries of animals fighting.

"Did you hear that?" Eugene whispered.

"Let's get to the car," Bill responded.

Before they could move, they heard the crackling sound of brush crushed underfoot. A large cougar leaped onto the picnic table a few yards from where the boys lay with their muscles petrified and eyes transfixed. Swallowing their breath, they watched the mountain lion rummage through the bacon and eggs, scattering pans and plates in all directions. An eternity later, the headlights of a vehicle turning into the camp flashed on the cat. Startled, it leaped toward the boys, bounced off Bill's feet and disappeared into the woods.

"I told you we shouldn't put the food out," Bill said through chattering teeth. "I only listened to you because you said you'd camped out a lot with your family."

"We did," Eugene responded, "but nothing like this ever happened."

"Where did you go camping?"

Eugene cleared his throat before answering. "Hawaii."

If Bill had asked that question earlier, he would have had a better basis for evaluating his friend's judgment in the situation.

If you venture out with friends sailing, flying, backpacking or in some other potentially hazardous travel mode that you have little or no knowledge about, don't be afraid to ask questions.

"Where have you sailed before?"

"To the gas dock."

"I see. How often do you sail?"

"Often, because there's a leak in the gas tank."

"Is there a radio on board?"

"Why? So mother can call?"

"Then what do you do if a storm comes up?"

"Hide."

"Have you ever had any problems?"

"Just the time we ran into that oil tanker."

Sometimes friends are embarrassed to ask questions that convey a lack of trust or fainthearted spirit. Or, because they like and trust their friend's judgment in some nonrelated area like investments or cardiology, they assume the friend is trustworthy and capable in other areas as well. But brain surgeons have been known to crash their privately owned planes and high-court judges have had boating accidents. Such facts need not inhibit your spirit of adventure as long as you have enough information to make good travel decisions.

COURTESIES

You've traveled with friends and had a great time. You may wonder if you'll be invited again. Your friends may be wondering the same thing. Why not let them know with a telephone call or personal note how much you enjoyed being with them and how you would love to do it again.

When you've been someone's guest, be sure to write a thank-you note, pointing out the things you particularly enjoyed, and if you've stayed in their home, you may want to send a small thank-you gift.

Of course, you'll want to quickly pay any part of the trip owed or borrowed from your friends. It's a nice gesture too when you send copies of travel photographs you think they might enjoy having. You might even want to celebrate your experience with a reunion party.

After the trip to Africa I took with a group of travel agents, one husband and wife in our party hosted a reunion. Some travelers flew or drove long distances to be there. It was an opportunity to share photographs and the camaraderie developed during the safari—and an opportunity to wear all that safari garb we bought for the trip.

SIX

How to Survive Traveling with Your Kids

Advantages

A couple took their eight-year-old son, Michael, to the big island of Hawaii. After a five-hour flight from the mainland to Honolulu, they flew a connecting flight to Hilo and were picked up by a bus for a ride to Hawaii Volcanoes National Park. The tour was dragging over four hours because the loquacious bus driver stopped to explain every rock and leaf along the way. Finally, the driver-guide asked if there was anything else the tour group would like to see. A restless Michael shouted to the guide, "Why don't you just shut up and drive?" His parents were mortified. They chastised their son for his rudeness and told him that if he did anything like that again, they were going right home. When they finally got to the hotel, they insisted Michael apologize to the bus driver.

"My mom says I shouldn't yell 'shut up.' I'm really sorry. Next time I'll whisper," Michael told him.

Fortunately, even when you can't always predict your child's behavior, there are advantages to traveling with kids.

A mother called me last summer to change the annual family

vacation—she and her husband would be going without the kids. She was practically in tears. Her 16-year-old daughter had been selected to tour the United States with a renowned youth choir while her 15-year-old son had made the high-school football team and wouldn't miss preseason practice for all the Big Macs in America.

"That's terrific. So why are you so upset?" I asked.

"I can't believe the kids are already grown up and going their separate ways after only 15 years."

Though at times it seemed like an eternity, 15 years was not, in her mind, enough time. Her husband worked long hours, leaving little daily time for the children. He always looked forward to discovering his kids during these summer vacations. Now, at least one opportunity to get to know them better was lost.

The main advantage of traveling with kids, particularly if they don't live with you because of divorce, is the opportunity to bring the family closer together by sharing time and experiences. (And three or four people in a motel room with one bathroom provides plenty of closeness.)

Beyond that, it's a learning experience. The children learn how far they can torment each other before their parents explode and just how far "far" is to the next potty. Parents learn how to elicit cooperation (speak softly and carry a big stick) and how to remember all the sunglasses, cameras and teddy bears before they're left behind in motels and restaurants. Family travel is an exercise in how to accommodate others and enjoy it—and that's not bad training for the rest of life either.

In addition to developing social skills, travel opens up the world to your children, a world of beauty and wonder, of people and palaces, pleasures and possibilities. Their energy and enthusiasm for each new discovery is infectious and what makes traveling with the kids fun.

Disadvantages

You've probably noticed that a few days before you travel, you're busier than usual: running to stores to find a pair of comfortable walking shoes (Finding the lost ark would be easier!) or travel-size plastic bottles for suntan lotion and shampoo; collecting passports and visas (Why didn't someone tell you the Brazil consulate closes for lunch?); or interviewing plant sitters to talk to your rare-orchid collection. The additional time and energy required to get the kids ready for the trip is one of the disadvantages of family travel, at least until they can pack for themselves or chauffeur their parents to the consulate.

Another often-heard comment is "A vacation with the kids isn't a vacation. Eating in family restaurants along with other parents and their not-so-well-behaved kids is not relaxing, and we can't go anywhere at night." While family travel will place limits on parents' activities, these limitations can be minimized with proper planning.

The extra cost of traveling with the kids, however, is one disadvantage that can't be denied. It's not cheaper by the dozen. Rarely are airfares less for children. For most domestic travel, children over two years old will be charged the same fares as an adult, or at best, two-thirds of a nondiscounted adult airfare. While a few hotel chains allow children under 12 to stay free with their parents, many others charge extra for a child in the same room, and some limit the occupants of a hotel room to three. A family of five, then, will need at least two rooms or a suite, a larger rental car and, of course, a lot more munchies.

In other words, a one-week trip to Hawaii from the West Coast that costs $1,400 for two adults (excluding food) will cost $3,500 with three children. Because of the extra expenses, the family may have to limit travel to shorter periods at destinations closer to home.

You may accept the limitations on choices, the extra preparation and costs, but if the kids don't behave well with their siblings or stepsiblings, you might be tempted to pack them up and ship them home to Grandma. The more personalities and expectations to mesh, the more difficult it is to achieve harmony. It's hard to drive when the kids are boxing in the backseat, and it's hard to visit a museum when the five-year-old is crying she's tired and the eight-year-old twins are playing laser tag around the exhibits. But while traveling with the kids can be nerve-wracking, it's rarely boring and always a challenge.

TRAVELING WITH AN INFANT

Keep It Simple

The easiest trip you can make with an infant or small children is to a single destination like Grandma's or a self-contained resort. That way, you only have to carry the baby and all the support systems—bottles, formula, baby food, diapers, infant seat, stroller, toys—twice: coming and going.

A colleague used to hate the thought of packing and carrying all that "extra" paraphernalia until she realized that just as the parents had their suitcases, the baby was entitled to his. When she stopped thinking of it as "extra" packing, it became less of a labor. Carrying it, however, was still difficult, particularly when traveling alone with the baby.

Without someone else along to help with the load, traveling with an infant can be like swimming through wet cement. I once watched a young mother struggle through airport security with an infant in one arm and a garment bag over the other. Two bulging canvas bags hung from each shoulder along with a purse. When she bent to pick up the suitcase off the moving belt, the other bags fell off her shoulders and she had to stop and load up all over again. As she waddled toward a gate that must have seemed light years away, her purse fell again and I thought I heard a distinctive and understandable four-letter expletive. Other passengers might have helped had they not also been laden with carry-on luggage, cameras and kids.

Here are a few suggestions to help you through the airport if you're traveling alone with an infant:

1. Don't park your car at the airport, even if it's only for a day or two. You don't want to get on and off a shuttle from the parking lot or have to walk to the terminal. Have a cab or friend drop you off at the airport so you can check your luggage curbside with a porter and get rid of your bags right there or pay a porter to help you to the baggage counter.

2. Check everything you can in baggage. Getting in and out of the airport fast like a business executive is not the objective here. The objective is getting you and the baby to the gate in one piece.

3. Take short air hops so you can minimize the bottles and diapers you must take on board. If you're a woman, place your purse inside a larger flight bag with the bottles and diapers you must take on board. That way, you only have one bag to carry in addition to the baby. If Grandpa in London threatens to disown you forever if you don't bring the baby on the 12-hour flight, ask him to meet you halfway—New York, Montreal, etc.

4. If money is no object, you can take along a nanny. Or ask your travel agent about service companies that meet and greet VIPs, celebrities and celebrities-in-training for a fee. You don't have

to be a celebrity to hire the service; you only have to pay the fee, which can vary from $15 to $50 at each airport. By the way, none of these helpers is allowed in customs, so if you're flying in from an international point, you'll still have to manage your own luggage in customs.

5. If you haven't won the lottery yet and money is a factor, you can do what a divorced friend does. She pays her neighbor's 17-year-old son $15 plus gas to drive her to the airport and help her carry her hand luggage and the kids to the gate. She even gave him a title—her "Airport Assistance Rep." He loves feeling professional and loves the extra moola even more.

6. Love won't make your baby feel lighter on a half-mile trek to the gate. (Why is it always the very last gate?) A friend carries his baby in a backpack because it frees his hands. If a papoose clashes with your designer clothes, you might prefer to take a collapsible stroller that fits in the overhead compartment.

7. Try not to change planes, but if you must, make sure they are with the same carrier so you'll stay in the same terminal and won't have to ride shuttles around the airport.

By the way, you may have seen airline personnel zip passengers around in an electric cart and wondered how they got so lucky. Even a professional football punter whose foot insurance prohibits him from riding escalators or climbing stairs can't count on a cart. Many airlines don't have them, and even when requested in advance, somehow the cart is called to another gate just before you get there or the cart driver never answers the page.

If your destination is only a few hours away, you can avoid airports altogether and drive. If the baby cries, she's not disturbing anyone except her parents. If you must travel by plane, advise the reservationist that you are traveling with an infant and request your seat assignment at that time.

In the United States, children under the age of two travel free with an adult but are *not* entitled to a separate seat. The airlines will try, however, to leave the seat next to you open when you advise them you're traveling with an infant. If the flight is fully booked, this may not be possible. You'll have a better chance of finding an adjacent empty seat if you request seats in the middle section of a jumbo jet (DC10, 747, 767). Most travelers prefer to be seated next to a window or on the aisle and avoid the seats in the middle section where there are four or five seats across. On smaller jets, with two or three seats across on each side of a central aisle, you'll probably do best by requesting bulkhead seats. This is the first row of the section that faces a partition (bulkhead). Some airlines will not preassign these seats but dole them out at the airport specifically to handicapped passengers or passengers with small children. Frequent flyers avoid them for that reason—they don't want to sit next to fussing babies. Some bulkheads, usually on widebodies like DC10s, have hooks in the wall where the cabin crew can hang bassinets for babies up to a certain weight (which includes most babies up to about six months old). Request a bassinet when you make your reservations—there's usually no extra charge. Remember, however, that since there are no seats in front of you, items you would normally store under them will have to fit in an overhead compartment.

A flight attendant who has flown for 30 years says the biggest mistake mothers make is bringing enough baby food, diapers and toys to stock Noah's Ark. Most airlines will supply baby food if you order in advance. Here is a checklist of items you are likely to need. They should all fit in one bag:

1. Disposable diapers (enough for the duration of the flight). You can use air sickness bags to dispose of dirty diapers in the bathroom trash receptacle.

2. A bottle of baby's favorite formula and a bottle of juice to ease earaches on takeoff and landing. (Although you can usually

get refills for milk or juice on board, you'll want at least one bottle handy while you wait for takeoff or until the plane levels and cabin service begins.)

3. A change of clothes for you and the baby in case the baby spits up.

4. A couple of small toys for entertainment.

5. Acetaminophen, decongestant or other remedies you normally use at the first sign of illness.

6. If your baby is into the munching stage, a few crackers in a plastic bag to help keep the baby occupied during delays at the airport.

7. A pacifier.

By the way, if you're renting a car at your destination, request an infant car seat when you make your reservation.

And what do you do if your baby cries on the plane—not a petite coo, but a 50-decibel cry worthy of the Met, the kind that turns all heads your way and makes you wish you could disappear under the seat?

Some helpful passengers will try to soothe your baby with their own version of coochi-coochi-coo. Others, however, will give you a look that says "Can't you do something to keep that kid quiet?" Even though you wish desperately that you could, bottles, pacifiers and toys don't always work. Sometimes nothing works. You needn't feel self-conscious. Coping with crying is part of the art of traveling with an infant.

Where to Stay

If you're traveling to Aunt Betsy's, you probably don't have a choice of accommodations. You may have chosen a resort, however, that offers a variety of hotel rooms or condo-type apartments. Where the difference in rate is of little or no consequence, a condo generally offers the benefit of more space for a crib, a refrigerator and a stove for heating bottles or preparing other foods. On the other hand, hotels frequently offer more services including a variety of restaurants, activities and entertainment on the premises and access to trusted babysitters.

When choosing a resort for your vacation, look for a destination that combines condo accommodations with the amenities of a hotel resort. How do you find one? You can start with your travel agent or a number of travel books that feature assessments of family resorts. Here are some questions to ask before making reservations:

1. Is there a refrigerator in the room?
2. Are cribs available, and what is the extra charge, if any?
3. Can the staff arrange for reliable babysitters? How much do they charge? What are their ages?
4. Are there bellmen to help with luggage? (If you have an infant to carry, you don't want to haul luggage too.)
5. Is there a small grocery store and sundry shop on or near the premises for purchasing items like milk, juice or diapers?
6. Is there a family-style restaurant that welcomes children?
7. Is there a children's pool with life guards, children's play area, crafts or other supervised children's activities?

If the answer to most of the above is no, chances are the resort does not encourage children, even older ones, as guests. You won't want to stay there if the staff is not likely to be helpful.

Finding Time for Mom and Dad

Parents who can afford to take along a nanny on a trip to care for their child could just as easily arrange for that care at home while they're away. Why, then, do they take their infant with them? The answer I hear most often is "We would miss the baby too much." As a friend puts it, "Particularly now, when the baby is changing every day, we don't want to miss the moment when he first grabs his toes or the umbrella in my mai tai."

The friend in question can't afford a nanny. But he can afford to take along his 14-year-old niece who loves children and enjoys the vacation adventures with her aunt and uncle.

She's old enough to babysit and enjoys entertaining the baby when he's awake. Her help relieves the parents from giving the infant their constant attention.

Some couples take Grandma along. But be careful: not all grandmothers equate their title with "built-in babysitter." One young couple took Grandma and the baby to New York. Assuming they would have someone to look after the child at night, the couple purchased theater tickets in advance. When they mentioned it, Grandma said she was sorry but she had already made a date with an old college beau for the evening in question. The young couple stayed in while Grandma and her old friend enjoyed the theater tickets.

If you don't have a relative or hired help, you can make time for yourself by taking turns. Mom can take care of the baby while Dad plays a round of golf and Dad can take over so Mom can spend a few hours in the spa. That way, both parents will have an opportunity to enjoy the reosrt facilities. Some couples even make a list of the activities they want to try so each will know in advance when to expect their turn as "watch commander."

And for a candlelight dinner together at a fine restaurant or a night of dancing under the stars, you can arrange for a babysitter. This way, you might not have as much leisure time as you'd like, but it's probably still more than you'd have at home.

VACATIONING WITH TODDLERS

Unlike infants, who sleep most of the day and are relatively immobile and undemanding, toddlers (ages one to about two) are children whose energy spurts can rival a high-speed train while their comprehension of "no" is still not quite on-line. Toddlers are like wind-up toys: you can't be sure which direction they'll go or what they'll bump into. Some parents wouldn't dream of traveling with them. But it's not a matter of courage as much as organization.

Easiest Trips

One of the easiest trips with toddlers is to a destination resort that provides supervised fun for small children.

Club Med, for example, has mini-clubs at several of its resorts where children ages two to seven can play games, build sand castles, learn arts and crafts and eat together under staff supervision, leaving their parents free to play games, build sand castles, learn arts and crafts and eat in the company of other adults. At selected resorts, Club Med also has baby clubs—supervised nurseries complete with cribs and playpens—for infants from four months to two years of age.

Some cruise ships also provide supervision for children ages six months and up. Parents, however, are still responsible for changing diapers and feeding their children.

You don't have to take a cruise or leave the country to find a resort that offers day care. A colleague recently took his one-year-old daughter to Aspen, Colorado. Each morning he took the free shuttle bus to the day-care center and dropped off his daughter before hitting the slopes with his friends. The baby cried the first day—she didn't want to leave Daddy. By the third day, however, she ran into the center without looking back.

What if you can't afford a full-service resort but need a change of scenery? A couple in Los Angeles takes a vacation each summer with two small children. Since they can't afford to fly anywhere, they drive 30 minutes to Malibu and stay at a motel on the beach for three weeks. During the day, the kids play at a nearby day-care center the couple found by placing a few telephone calls to friends who live in the area. This way, Dad still has a vacation from his job, Mom doesn't have to cook three meals a day and the children look forward to seeing the friends they played with the previous year. And if one gets sick, they're only 30 minutes from the pediatrician.

Dining Out with Toddlers

The moment you dress some toddlers in their fancy clothes, they suddenly know how to sit still and eat like an adult (well, almost). Consequently, you can take them to a fine restaurant and feel confident that your dinner will remain on the table long enough for you to eat. Some small fry, however, perceive the place settings on an elegant table as another set of blocks that must pass their personal stress test before insertion in their mouths. Attempts to dissuade them from grabbing and throwing such fascinating objects as Lenox teacups and Waterford goblets can result in wails of frustration.

Where you dine with toddlers will depend somewhat on the personalities and behavior of your children, but if they resemble the latter type, you can take them to a family diner or fast-food restaurant, where restless children don't raise an eyebrow. Parents who long for an elegant dinner can take their children for an early meal and leave them with a babysitter before sampling chateaubriand amid tuxedoed waiters with French accents.

Picnics are an easy way to eat during the day. It doesn't matter if the kids make a mess outdoors. With the use of paper cups and plates, cleanup time can be kept to a minimum. All you need is a local convenience store or deli and a refrigerator (so you can store any mayonnaise and catsup not left on the kids' clothes).

Leaving Favorite Things Behind

I was almost four years old when our family set out on our first cross-country trip from Cleveland to Los Angeles. While my parents were occupied loading suitcases and snacks into the car, I quietly piled my stuffed animals into the backseat. All went well until my brother blew the whistle.

"Mom, Dee Dee's taking up all the space in the backseat with her toys and they're on *my side* of the car."

What ensued was pure anguish as I watched my eleven "friends" forcibly removed from the positions I'd lovingly arranged. I screamed. I cried. I ranted, raved and tugged. "You can take *one*," I was told finally. In the face of overwhelming opposition, it was enough of a concession to shut me up. I chose "Old Bunny," my favorite. (Later, when I discovered "Old Bunny" wasn't a bunny at all, but a bear, it didn't lessen my affection for him.)

Sometimes, children want to take *all* their toys on a trip simply because they don't understand they will be coming back. Whatever the reason, trauma can sometimes be avoided by having your child choose one or two favorite things in advance of the trip and letting them get used to the idea.

"And which one are you going to bring, Andy?" you ask.

You know you're in trouble when Andy drags out his 12-foot-square Snoopy blanket, dog-eared in more ways than one. A discourse on airline baggage limitations is unlikely to lessen his attachment to the blanket, but you can try the power of suggestion.

"Sweetheart, why don't you take Mickey Mouse?" (or any toy that's easy to pack) you might say. "See how he fits in your suitcase?"

If Mickey Mouse fails to replace the blanket in the child's

heart, there's another tactic. Buy a new, smaller version of his favorite thing, such as a two-foot-square blanket, with the explanation that one is for the house and the other is for traveling. And cross your fingers he doesn't insist on the *old* blanket.

On the Way

Tots can't be expected to sit still for several hours. Sometimes, however, parents can't avoid long trips. A friend who lives in Eugene, Oregon, occasionally drives to Los Angeles to visit her mother. She takes a route that allows her to stop along the way to visit friends who also have small children. She lets her children stay up later than usual playing with friends, and the next day, she drives in peace while they sleep in the car. She also brings a grab bag of surprise toys or treats to give them at intervals along the way. If the kids don't behave, they lose their turn at the "Surprise Box."

If you don't have friends along your route, you can still plan frequent stops—a park with swings, a zoo, a pony ride—to prevent the irritable behavior that comes from boredom. If it's raining, a walk through an enclosed shopping mall can help disperse pent-up energy and give the children something to look forward to along the way. Just don't be surprised if your wallet gets some exercise too.

While train and boat travel allow some opportunity for movement, the main exercise you get on a plane is to and from the lavatory (if you're lucky enough not to have the aisle blocked by meal or drink carts at the moment of need). Toys don't occupy toddlers long before they need to crawl, climb or waddle. For this reason, many parents prefer to book night flights. There's a chance the kids will sleep even if their parents don't, and as these flights are less desirable, you can often find two or three empty seats together for additional crawling space. (Caution: if your children tend to cry a lot when they're tired, your fellow passengers on the red-eye may really see red.)

Some parents enlist older children to help with smaller ones. A client flew with his two-year-old son and four-year-old daughter to the East Coast to visit his family. On the flight to New York, the older child quietly entertained herself with coloring books until her pesky little brother began grabbing her crayons, at which point, a noisy tug of war began with Dad as constant referee. Before their return, the client spoke to his daughter and asked for her "help" in handling the younger child on the flight home because she was "grown up." This time, instead of demonstrating her annoyance with her sibling, she helped him scribble on paper with her crayons. From then on, the client decided that "good management practices" like asking instead of telling could also apply to his children.

When Three Is Less Than Two

Because children under age two can fly free domestically with an adult, many parents try to pass off toddlers as infants. The problem with this savings plan is that infants are not entitled to seats. On a crowded flight to Florida, I once watched parents struggle with two "infants" who were either well over two or destined for careers in professional basketball. At lunchtime, the father fed the mother with a spoon from his meal tray while she held both tots. Later, when she had to get out of her seat, it required 10 minutes of maneuvering. I'm sure they concluded that four bodies stuffed into two seats wasn't worth the savings. Even if your child is under two, you may want to pay a child's fare to be sure of a seat. If money is a problem, at least avoid traveling on holidays and the height of the travel season when you're unlikely to find empty seats.

Organizing the Day

How you arrange to keep toddlers busy at your destination will depend on their personalities. Some children may be content to look at picture books or play with blocks for hours. Others need to run, climb or crawl. Whatever your children's natures, you should allow for physical play time as well as quiet time. A daily plan that includes play and quiet time for Mom and Dad might look like this:

8 A.M.	Breakfast in the condo at the resort.
9 A.M.	Quiet play time or cartoon watching for the children while Mom and Dad get ready for the day.
10 A.M.	Pool time for the whole family. Introduce kids to the water. (Don't forget sunblock and hats.)
11 A.M.	Dad takes kids back to condo for quiet play time while Mom goes to the spa.
12 NOON	Lunch at a casual restaurant.
1 P.M.	Nap time for tots and rest time for parents.
3 P.M.	Children play on swings and in sandbox (supervised by hotel staff) while Mom and Dad play tennis.
5 P.M.	Family nature walk before dinner.
6 P.M.	Dinner.
8 P.M.	Children stay with babysitter while parents go dancing, to a movie or make love on the beach.

If the children will be staying up for a while with a babysitter who is unfamiliar with them, be sure to leave a few familiar toys, games or books for the children.

VACATIONING WITH SCHOOL-AGE CHILDREN

Where to Go—Four Family Favorites

SEE AMERICA

By the time I was 13, our family had crossed the country between Cleveland and Los Angeles by car eight times. I remember those trips, made at an impressionable age, more vividly than many recent ones: the great red rawness of the Grand Canyon in Arizona and the outhouse that came with our cabin that night; in New Mexico, the mysterious Carlsbad Caverns and the stoic faces of native Americans gathering the meager remnants of a corn crop after a flash flood; the muddy might of the Mississippi; the green of Kentucky's "blue grass" and the bounteous endowment of America's breadbasket states.

And I can remember the songs of those days, songs on the radio that accompanied us through Missouri, Indiana and Illinois, songs we sang along to through Texas and Tennessee. And who could forget the Burma Shave jingles on signs along the highways. Travel across the states was a lesson in Americana.

When our car broke down (and it always broke down somewhere) in a rural hamlet of Arkansas, I met some children, all blondes about my age. They stared at us wide-eyed because they had never seen black hair before. And I marveled at the homogeneous nature of some small towns.

Seeing America can be more than a geography lesson and an introduction to its cities and natural wonders. It can be an awakening to the country's cohesion and diversity, a lesson in sociology, encapsuled in a few days' time but forever embedded in memory—lessons you don't want your kids to miss.

A SUMMER PLACE

What do you do if the family doesn't fit in one car? With six children ranging in age from 6 to 15, the Anderson family totals eight. Even with a full-size station wagon, they can't travel with luggage comfortably on a prolonged road trip. So whenever they can, the Andersons take the train. Not only is it relaxing, but they also save on family-plan transportation—children ages 2 to 15 pay 50 percent of the adult fare, and children under age 2 are free. Although train lines don't go everywhere in the United States, they still reach numerous destinations.

A favorite summer place with easy train access is a ranch in Colorado. The Andersons take the train from Chicago to Winter Park, where a van from a nearby ranch meets them and transfers them to their three-room, two-bath cottage. Once there, the children go their separate ways—the older kids sign up for river rafting and trail rides, while the younger boys play cowboys, swim or fish. The 7-year-old daughter enjoys the swings and Navajo beadwork. The ranch also offers tennis, fishing, racquetball, canoeing, organized hikes, hay rides, square dancing and sing-alongs. Mom and Dad join in the fun or just hang out in a hammock. Even dining is easy. The children know their Mom and Dad will have lunch at noon and dinner at six in the restaurant. The kids can join them or eat with their new friends.

Families who prefer water sports can find similar variety at a beach or lake resort.

VISITING RELATIVES

Many families spend their vacations visiting relatives scattered across the country. For some, staying with relatives is the only way to afford a vacation. An added advantage is having uncles, aunts, cousins or grandparents around to help entertain parents and children alike.

After moving to California, our family returned each summer to Cleveland, where my brother and I had 18 first cousins and hundreds of second and third cousins. We had no need to look outside the family for entertainment. With so many relatives, there was always a wedding, birthday or anniversary to celebrate and always someone to play with. The older kids organized the younger ones into a "big show" with singing, dancing and skits and charged parents a few cents' admission. For us kids, summer was nonstop fun mainly because of the presence of other children our own age.

Visiting your Aunt Betsy, Uncle John or Grandma might be okay for a day or two, but after that, some children can become bored without other children around. Try to include "kid" activities—visits to amusement parks, movies, swimming—or follow the visit to the relatives with a tour of Disneyland or other place with "kid appeal." You want your child to have something to look forward to and some enthusiasm when the teacher assigns the inevitable "What I did for summer vacation" essay.

A WINTER HOLIDAY

The Corwin family vacations each winter at a ski resort. Because they all ski at different levels, the five family members don't always ski together. The 12-year-old, for example, can leave his parents in a cloud of powder and join an advance ski class to take on more challenging slopes, while his three-year-old sister might have a short beginner lesson and spend the rest of the day building a snowman at the day-care center.

The kids have opportunities to meet other kids in classes and lift lines, and the activities don't end there. Major resorts like Vail in Colorado also offer snowmobiling, ice skating, cross-country skiing, sleigh rides and ballooning. And if the weather takes an angry turn, the youngsters can play racquetball, take aerobic classes or swim. They can eat in, eat out, watch television, play cards, read, go to a movie or massage their aches and pains in the sauna or Jacuzzi at their rented condo.

If all of this seems too wonderful, check the costs carefully. A cartoon posted on a ski school bulletin board read: "The most important aerobic exercise you can do to get ready for ski season is opening and closing your wallet."

In addition to transportation, housing and meals, you have to figure in the costs of equipment purchase or rental, lift tickets, lessons and ski clothes. And don't forget accident insurance. On the plus side, you never have that What-do-we-get-the-kids-for-Christmas dilemma. While your kids are growing in size and ability, you never finish replacing clothes and equipment.

If you'd like to get your family into skiing, or any other sport, but are afraid of high costs, ask your travel agent to compare packages that include transportation, accommodations, transfers and lift tickets. Resorts vary. At Vail in Colorado, for example, children's lift tickets are about two-thirds the adult price. At Mt. Bachelor in Oregon, however, children under 12 pay about half while children under 6 ski free on weekdays.

One of the best ways for a family to vacation together is to share a sport like tennis, snorkeling, kayaking or skiing. If your family doesn't have a sport you all enjoy, try to find one. Vacation planning can be simplified when you all love the same activity.

Dining

What can you do if little Joey eats only hamburgers?

One couple lets their kids take turns picking restaurants. Scott, at age six, the youngest of the children, always picks McDonald's, which his sister Lori hates because, having a wheat allergy, she can't eat the buns. She stopped complaining because she doesn't want to hear him squawk when she picks her favorite French restaurant. "Our only real problem," says their mom, Katie, "is Ricky's night. Ever since he did a social studies report on Japan for his eighth grade class, he's been hooked on sushi. That's the one night we still have to stop on the way home to pick up Scott's hamburger."

Some lessons were learned the hard way. One evening, says Katie, the family was already munching on bread and drinking at Lori's restaurant choice in San Francisco when they realized the prices on the menu were way over their budget. "Embarrassed to tell the waiter, we quietly walked out and left our eight-year-old, Susan, to tell the waiter we didn't have enough money. After all, who could get peeved at a cute little pixie in pigtails? I still think it's a good idea to involve the kids in the dining selection, but now, Dick and I pre-screen the restaurant list for prices."

Other frequent family travelers offer these tips: When time is important in your schedule, try to hit restaurants in the off-peak hours so you don't have to wait for a table. Snacking between meals can alleviate irritability as well as hunger pangs and allow you to eat a lighter, quicker meal in the restaurant. If your children have sensitive stomachs, try to keep their diet similar to meals at home to lessen the possibility that they'll develop stomachaches or throw up.

Learning to Pack

A client packed her seven-year-old's suitcase for a trip to Disneyland. A few days later, her son asked if he could bring some toys. She said, "Only if they fit in your suitcase without making it bulge. Otherwise, the suitcase will break."

When they arrived in Los Angeles, she was shocked when she opened his suitcase. It was filled with toy cars and trucks, but there wasn't a stitch of clothing. "Gerald, what did you do with your clothes?"

"Mommy, you said the suitcase would break if there was a lump in it. When I put the toys in, the clothes made a lump, so I took them out."

As Gerald's mother rushed him to the department store, she wondered where she had gone wrong. She didn't know if she should be angry or laugh at his misinterpretation of her instructions. But she was determined not to make the same mistake again. She began training him to pack for himself. First she gave him a list of clothes to find and place on his bed. When he had assembled everything, she showed him how to place them in the suitcase, explaining why he would need each item—his bathing suit for the pool, his long pants for the nice restaurant—and then she let him finish. When she inspected his job, she noticed that he had added a few "extras" not on the list and the suitcase wouldn't close.

"Okay, you'll have to take something out. What'll it be?" she asked him. He reached for his sweater and then hesitated, as if remembering why he would need it. Finally, he removed one of the toys he had added. Mission accomplished. Now all they had to work on was the difference in meaning between "place neatly" and "wad into balls."

Some parents prefer to pack for their kids because they want it done right. But kids can learn something from making the wrong decisions too, particularly when they have to live with those decisions for a whole week. And once they learn how to pack, they'll be able to make up their own packing lists when they know the parameters of the trip. Developing this skill takes discussion. After all, even adults have difficulty determining what to pack at times. One family makes a game out of it. Whoever comes up with the shortest list wins a prize. Of course, if they leave off an essential item like underwear or eyeglasses, they lose points. They also lose points for superfluous items like ice skates and cowboy hats. They make up their lists at least two weeks in advance so there will be time to shop for missing items or replace worn-out ones.

Involve the Kids in Planning

Before my family's first trip to California, I had a strange conception of geography. The world, according to this four-year-old, was a straight line with colder countries like Sweden at one end and warmer ones at the opposite end. California was way out there at the warm end while Cleveland was just a few places removed from the North Pole. Imagine my surprise the first time my father laid out the map of the United States on the floor so we kids could trace Route 66 in red crayon. We pored over the map for weeks, convinced that the task of getting to the Pacific Ocean fell squarely on our shoulders as we drew circles around the cities that marked the way.

Besides an enlightening lesson in geography, working with the map eliminated the need to badger our parents with that infamous road question, "When are we going to get there?"

We knew precisely when we would get there because we had our own maps to follow. Alternating the task of navigator, we took delight in proclaiming, "Okay, switch to Highway 22 at the next town," or "Turn left at the next signal."

If you're not driving to your destination, you can still familiarize your children with their vacation place by showing them maps of the area, brochures and other promotional information obtainable from travel agencies, chambers of commerce and government tourist offices. Involving them in the planning can heighten the excitement and make them feel they are contributing to the success of the trip. And the more they do, the less you'll have to do.

Before a trip, like the one they took through Washington, D.C., and Virginia, friends assign a different list to each member of the family. Ron, the oldest at age 15, lists the sights to see along the way, including museums and historical houses, noting the hours they're open for viewing and any cost. Of course, the parents check the list for feasibility. The one time they didn't, they ended up 200 miles out of their way just to see where Davy Crockett slept.

The two younger children make a list of items to take: alarm clock, maps, picnic basket, playing cards. (See packing suggestions in appendix A.) The parents have their own lists: Dad is in charge of the car list, e.g., checking the condition of windshield wipers, tires, flares, flashlight, first-aid kit, tools and road maps. Mom assembles the family medicines, eyeglass prescriptions, addresses and telephone numbers that might be needed along the way and takes care of the travel documents.

It's a good idea to keep a master list in a file labeled with the date and destination of the trip. Staple the list inside and check off items as they are handled:

__ Airline tickets	__ Plants
__ Hotels reserved	__ Pet sitter
__ Deposits sent	__ Mail handled
__ Travelers checks	__ House security
__ Foreign currency	__ Car checked
__ Cash	__ Passports
__ Packing	__ Bills paid
__ Visas	__ Newspapers stopped
__ Inoculations	__ Car checked
__ Snacks	__ Emergency numbers left with neighbors

The next time you travel to a similar climate, you can pull out the old lists and simply update them. In fact, you should keep all data related to the same trip (tickets, hotel deposit receipts, packing lists, etc.) in the same file. This way you'll never experience the panicky feeling that comes when you can't remember what you did with the tickets.

Discuss Behavior—What's Expected

A father who drives his family 400 miles to their vacation home explains that there will be only two stops en route. Knowing this in advance, the children adjust their timing and liquid intake accordingly.

The first time the couple took their children to a museum, they pulled the kids aside before going in—an indication that what they were about to say was important. "If you want to say something, remember to whisper and never, never touch the paintings or walls."

Before a trip, or any new experience, explain what behavior is expected. If you're taking a road trip, for example, putting the "rules of the road" on paper will give them added emphasis. Here's a sample of one family's list:

1. Bathroom stops will be made at three-hour intervals.

2. The following messy foods are not permitted in the car:

   • sunflower seeds, peanuts or other nuts that need shelling

   • ice cream cones (On the previous trip, the top scoop had fallen off the seven-year-old's cone and down his father's neck while he was driving, sending both the car and the father into a skid.)

   • donuts with powdered sugar

   • spiders or other bugs to torment siblings and parents

3. Seat belts will be fastened at all times.

4. All trash will be placed in the litter bag and nothing thrown out the window.

5. No arms, feet or other body parts shall be hung out the windows.

6. All problems and complaints will be settled by the arbitrator (Mom or Dad), whose decisions are final and not subject to appeal.

7. No fighting.

It's important, however, to follow through on the laws you lay down. A friend stopped en route to her destination at a restaurant for dinner with her three daughters. Soon, one was kicking her sister who was crawling around under the table while the third was crying. Although their food had just been served, the mother paid the bill and marched the girls out of the restaurant. "They knew I was dead serious. They learned that if they misbehaved, they would miss their dinner and the ice cream sundaes they had looked forward to. I never had the problem again. It's an inconvenience to terminate an activity or trip when you've gone through a lot of effort to plan it, but you have to follow through with no second chances or you set yourself up for trouble." Of course your "or elses" should be realistic so you *can* follow through.

When we were young, my brother had a habit of sleeping in the car on our cross-country trips. He stretched out the full length of the backseat as if being two years older were tantamount to absolute power. While I perched uncomfortably on a corner of the seat, my protests grew until they escalated into war somewhere outside Cheyenne. My father stopped the car abruptly and said, "If you two don't behave, we'll turn around and go back right now."

If we didn't believe him, we knew enough to pretend we did. Silently, we sat back, comfortable in the knowledge that the "turn-around-and-go-back" threat was an idle one. Still, it had a certain dramatic quality. We were quiet for at least 20 minutes.

If there's no place in the front seat to separate siblings, a solution might be to set a line of demarcation in the car so children don't encroach on the other's "space."

Keeping Them Busy

Crossing through the farm states was a testy time. At the first sight of cows in a pasture, we would stick our heads out the window to moo. When these attempts at provocation evoked only unblinking stares from heifers that seemed to say "Oh, grow up," we sat back to face miles of monotonous farms.

This would be a critical time to start a game. Here are a few of the time-honored favorites that require only paper and pencil.

1. *The license plate game*—Everyone tries to spot license plates from as many states as possible. The advantage of this game is that it can be a group effort and not likely to provoke aggressive or argumentative behavior that sometimes develops from more competitive games. If, however, there are few cars on the road, you may want to switch to another game or take a nap.

2. *The alphabet game*—Everyone tries to spot names of restaurants, stores, towns, etc., along the roadside that begin with the next letter of the alphabet. This is not the right game for traveling through Death Valley, California, or Denali National Park in Alaska, where signs and humans are few.

3. *The travel game*—One person says something like, "I'm going to Timbuktu and I'm taking my camel." The next person has to repeat what the first person said and add a new item: "I'm going to Timbuktu and I'm taking a camel and an ice cream machine." As items get added, it becomes more difficult to repeat all the items in order. Anyone who forgets an item in the sequence is out of the game.

4. *Twenty questions*—Passengers take turns thinking of an animal,

mineral or vegetable. The other travelers try to discover what it is by asking no more than twenty questions.

5. *Progressive story*—One passenger begins a story with one sentence. The others continue the story by adding one sentence each. It may be ended any time and each person has a chance to begin a story.

If your car has a tape player and your children enjoy stories, you can bring audio cassettes with the companion books and a cassette player with head phones. This way, the kids can listen and follow along by themselves or the whole family can listen. The parents of an eight-year-old boy gave him a synthesizer for his birthday. With headphones attached to it, he can "rock out" in the car or airplane without disturbing anyone else with his music.

Games like checkers or Scrabble, which can be purchased in travel versions (a magnetic board keeps the pieces from slipping off), or card games (plastic cards are easier to wipe clean if food spills on them) are best for the plane, bus or other public conveyance because they're less verbal and don't require team participation.

Another way to keep children occupied is by assigning responsibilities appropriate for their ages and abilities.

In the Rossini family, Dad drives and pays the bills; Mom regulates snacks and watches for places of interest described in the guide books; Meg is the navigator, responsible for keeping them on the right road; Billy keeps an eye out for important signs like Construction Ahead and keeps track of the luggage pieces, making sure they all make it back into the car; and Molly, the youngest at age eight, checks under the beds in the motel rooms for personal items before they depart.

Keeping children busy also means including activities children enjoy. A friend, Lisa, was finishing her thesis for a master's degree in contemporary art and planned a combined vacation/study trip on the East Coast that included museums she needed to visit for her thesis. At the first museum, the children, ages 10 and 9, followed her around waiting for the fun to begin. Uninterested in what to them resembled the kindergarten drawings that once hung on the refrigerator door at home, they concluded that the large, almost empty gallery rooms were perfect for turning cartwheels. A few angry reprimands induced boisterous protests, and before Lisa could collect her information, the security guard asked them to leave.

"I was embarrassed and mad at the kids, but it was my fault. I thought they would develop an appreciation for art. They weren't ready. Still, I had a thesis to write and would not have another opportunity to make this trip. I needed a place to park them. Since they had never been ice skating, I signed them up for a two-hour private lesson at a local rink. After that, all I had to do was drop them off at the rink, which was in a nice shopping mall, while I went to the museum. By the end of the trip, I had my data and they were pretty good skaters."

Motorcoach Tours

I've booked many families with school-age children on bus tours of places such as Canada, China and Europe. Some families prefer motorcoach tours, particularly if traveling in a country where they feel uncomfortable on their own, because they don't have to do much planning or deal with a foreign language.

Before signing up for a motorcoach tour, be sure you consider these factors:

Cost: Some tours can cost the same or less than traveling on your own. Others can cost more. If cost is a concern, you may want to weigh one mode of travel against the other. When you add the costs of traveling on your own, be sure to consider accommodations including tax, service charges and tips to bellhops, as well as meals, entrance fees to museums and parks and transportation. If you will need a rental car, include the costs of gas, taxes, insurance, parking and tolls. Check for drop-off charges if leaving the car in a different city from where you originate.

How will your children react? Do your children behave well around strangers? Some behave better around unfamiliar faces. Or will they be running up and down the aisles of the motorcoach irritating their fellow passengers? Do they function well when their activities are highly structured? Do they like travel enough to trek around ruins all day or watch scenery from a bus seat?

How will you react? Even if the tour is perfect for your children, what about you? Are you the type who hates schedules and sightseeing? Are you embarrassed to reprimand your children in front of others?

If you haven't tried a motorcoach tour because you don't know if the family will like it, start with a one-day side trip (from Washington, D.C., to Williamsburg, for example). Then try a two- or three-day trip before signing up for a week or more.

VACATIONING WITH TEENAGERS

The father of two teenagers called me to plan a summer vacation for the family. He and his wife were thinking about a cruise to Alaska but couldn't seem to interest the kids. Both were teenagers in high school and reluctant to miss out on summer beach parties and other activities with their friends.

I suggested they might need something more adventurous than a cruise to entice the kids. Instead of a 10-day cruise, we outlined an adventure trip to Alaska that included hiking, river rafting and horseback riding. At the end of the vacation, the kids would fly home and their parents would take a four-day cruise.

Two days later, the client told me the kids not only agreed to the trip, but they also decided as long as they were going, they may as well take the cruise too.

Adventure isn't necessarily the ingredient required to entice teenagers to travel with their parents, but it worked in this case because the kids had heard their peers talk about rafting and hiking trips.

Small children rarely have preconceived expectations about travel and are, therefore, rarely disappointed. Even airline food with its mini-packaging can be an adventure. Teenagers, however, may already have notions about what constitutes fun. For some, it may be nothing more than the opportunity to meet other teenagers, preferably of the opposite sex. It may be the promise of some physical challenge or the fascination with a different culture.

Often, places with teenage appeal are only a zip code away. Within an hour or two of Los Angeles, for example, both the desert town of Palm Springs and the seaside community of Balboa Island used to attract large numbers of teenagers in search of each other. During school breaks, however, thousands of teenagers made these "in" spots infamous for rowdiness and law-breaking, causing authorities to impose curfews and the teenagers to move on to other places. You'll want to avoid such spots, particularly when school is out. You are, however, competing with your teenagers' other activity choices and your destination should appeal to young people.

The key is to include your teenagers as much as possible in the decision making. In one family, everyone anonymously tosses his or her destination suggestion into a hat. The choices are pulled out one by one and discussed. Often, two or more family members come up with the same suggestion.

What do you do when you have small children as well as teenagers who don't want to be caught dead in a place full of younger children? Some friends send their eight-year-old to camp while they take the older kids to Club Med. Later, they take a separate trip with the younger boy and one of his friends. And if they do all travel together, they rarely ask the teenager to babysit his brother.

As your kids mature, they develop tastes and opinions of their own and you'll want their input on where to stay and where to dine. Tell them how much money you've allotted for the trip and let them learn how to pick hotels and restaurants within that budget.

The Goodwins prefer to travel with their teenage children, who have the ability and agility to do what their parents can't. "When we go skiing, it's our son, Tom, who gets under the car to put the chains on. My husband would throw his back out. Tom's a big help on our sailboat too. Susan, who's seventeen, does most of the driving. I'm glad she loves to drive so I don't have to. Now that they're teenagers, travel is a snap. And it's fun to have enterprising and energetic people around you."

It's important, however, that a vacation not become all work and no play for the kids. "Assuming you trust them," says Erika, a mother of three teenagers, "you should give them their space. We give them each a small amount of spending money on the trip and it's up to them to use it wisely. If they spend it all on video games and don't have any left for the movies or souvenirs, that's a choice they have to live with.

"We let them go places we think they can handle on their own. Spending time with us older folks is always an option, but we don't want it to be a requirement. Naturally, if they want to hang out at a local dance place, we do some reconnaissance first, to be sure it's a decent place. They're lucky they have each other for company, but they also have the responsibility of keeping an eye on each other.

"Of course, we have one way of making sure they choose to spend some time with us. When they go where we go, their father pays their way. If they want to save money, they stick close to the folks. As my daughter tells her daddy, 'Why should I leave you at the height of your earning capacity?'"

140

When They Fall in Love on the Road

I booked a couple and their two teenagers on a trip to Egypt and Greece. During a stopover in London, the daughter, age 17, fell in love with a local boy before they flew on to Cairo. Exciting as Egypt was, she pined the whole week so much that her father canceled their Greek island cruise, with considerable losses in prepayments, to return to London so his daughter could spend time with her new friend.

The girl had been plump through high school. Shy and self-conscious, she had missed out on most social activities and interaction with boys. With great effort, she had slimmed down before the trip with the family. Her father felt that the self-confidence gained by having the English fellow interested in her far outweighed the loss of advance deposits he had made in Greece.

Other parents frown on altering plans to accommodate teenage romance. As one mother puts it, "When my son falls in love, it's like an earthquake—it shakes him up, but it's over very quickly."

There are no set rules to follow when your kids fall in love on the road. How you react will depend on them and the circumstances. Although falling in love on vacation can fill your teenagers with special memories while filling you with anxiety, ultimately they will probably learn another important lesson of the road: A long-distance romance is difficult to maintain and after it's over, life, like the train, goes on to the next stop. The girl who fell in love in London wrote to her new friend for several months until she met a boy closer to home and, somehow, no longer had time for letter writing.

SEVEN

How to Travel with Someone Else's Kids

Advantages

If I could have traveled with anyone as a child, I would have chosen Auntie Mame. What fun it would have been to join this disarming character in the escapades described by her nephew, Patrick Dennis, in *Around the World with Auntie Mame.*

Like Auntie Mame, you don't need kids of your own to treat a child to the world of travel. All you need is the financial means and the desire to enrich someone else's life, whether nephew or neighbor.

The feeling you get from sharing your time and experiences with someone else's kids is the main advantage of taking them along. And if you have children of your own, they will have the added fun of company their own age. Instead of constantly entertaining them, you can watch the kids entertain each other while at the same time, they learn to share and get along with other personalities.

Disadvantages

A single client in his thirties wanted to take his niece and nephew to Acapulco. Then he began to worry. What if they get sick? What if they drown or have an accident while playing? What if there's an earthquake while we're there? How could he ever face their parents? He decided it was too much responsibility and went alone.

Along with extra responsibilities are the additional costs of transportation, rooms and meals. And you can't even claim any dependent deductions.

You'll have to commit more time to preparation too, coordinating with the children or their parents on what to pack and what to expect. But the disadvantage you may feel the most is the limits on your mobility and activities, particularly if traveling with small fries.

One mother who books her family's travel never schedules a flight before 10 A.M. because it takes several hours to get her three kids organized and out the door. When her kids' friends join them, she schedules flights after noon. The more kids along, the more bodies to move, the more time required to find misplaced shoes and wayward space rockets. When the head count is over four, she keeps flights to a minimum to spend less time organizing and more time having fun.

Unless you're accustomed to traveling with children, you may have to alter your usual activities and pass up the Folies Bergère for an evening of puppet theater. Fortunately, many adults accept the added responsibilities and disadvantages to give someone's kids and themselves a travel experience they might otherwise miss.

CONSIDERATIONS

Enthusiasm notwithstanding, there are factors to consider when traveling with someone else's kids that you don't have to think about with your own.

Children of Divorced or Separated Parents

The eight-year-old daughter of a client invited a classmate to join her family on a trip to Canada. The girl's mother gave her approval. When they crossed the international border from Vancouver on the road back to Seattle, their car was overtaken by a highway patrol vehicle with sirens blaring. The girl's father, angry that his daughter had been taken out of the country in violation of a custody agreement, had notified the highway patrol that his daughter had been kidnapped. Although the matter was straightened out, it provided some frightening moments for the family as well as the little friend.

If you're traveling with the children of divorced or separated parents, be sure to inquire about the "other" parent's consent. If the other parent's whereabouts are unknown, have the legal guardian provide written permission to take the child with you. In fact, a single parent cannot fly to Mexico with a child without the written consent of the other parent or legal proof of sole custody or that the other birth parent is either deceased or nowhere to be found.

Dennis the Menace

Before you suggest your children invite a friend on your vacation, think about whom they might ask. If you don't approve of all their friends, you'll want to narrow the selection or name someone specifically. If you say, "Susan, would you like to bring Marybeth along?" you won't get stuck with Dennis the Menace. Even if you trust your child's judgment, be sure both of you have spent enough time with the selected friend to make a good judgment.

The parents of a 14-year-old boy had hosted his bicycle club on numerous occasions and liked all the boys. When their son suggested inviting the newest member on their weekend outing to get to know him better, his parents thought it was a nice gesture. To their dismay, the new kid behaved abominably—bullying the younger kids in the family, using foul language and picking fights with others. "Why did you invite that hellion?" his father wanted to know.

Their son shrugged. "I didn't know the only reason he joined our club was because he was kicked out of his last one."

If your kids want to invite friends you don't know well, invite them to dinner or spend some time together first so you can get better acquainted. That way you won't be surprised when your guest turns out to be a Hell's Angel in training.

When a 16-year-old boy asked his parents if he could bring his 15-year-old girlfriend along on their trip, his parents said no for a number of reasons. As his mother explained, "We didn't want to encourage any romantic involvement at their age or provide opportunities for deeper intimacy, especially in front of his brother and sister. We told him our trip was a *family* vacation when we could share special time with each other."

Another couple, however, did take their teenage son's girlfriend along. "Her family had been friends of ours for years, and our son, Greg, grew up with her," his mother said. "We were reasonably sure their relationship had not progressed beyond the hand-holding stage and she shared a room with our daughter, who was also her friend."

Once at Lake Arrowhead, however, Greg was distracted by a number of other young girls and began to ignore the girlfriend he'd brought. His parents sensed the girl's disappointment and unhappiness and they took their son aside.

"Debbie is your guest and you have a responsibility to see that she has a good time. If you didn't want that obligation, you should not have invited her."

"I'll never do that again," Greg said, and stuffed his pockets with telephone numbers for next summer.

If you're surprised when your kids ask if they can bring along a friend of the opposite sex, it may be the perfect time for a family discussion. As teenagers struggle to define their own values and goals, it's important they at least have a clear idea of their parents' expectations.

Spoiled Children

A couple and their six-year-old daughter, Jeannie, visited relatives in New York, where their daughter met her cousin, Abby, who was the same age. Jeannie's parents decided to take Abby along on their side trip to Nantucket so the girls could spend more time together.

When the cab pulled up at the Manhattan townhouse, Abby complained that taxis were dirty. "We always go to the airport in a limousine," she said.

"Mommy, what's a limousine?" Jeannie wanted to know.

In Nantucket, the parents had reserved a modest but cozy cottage.

"I'm hungry. Let's call room service," Abby said.

"Sorry, there's no room service here."

"We never stay anyplace that doesn't have room service," Abby proclaimed. "We stay in deluxe hotels."

"Daddy, can we stay in a deluxe hotel too?" Jeannie asked, eager to please her new friend.

Abby wanted to buy everything in the shops. "I want the teddy bear, please."

"I want a teddy bear too, Daddy," Jeannie imitated.

The parents decided that the cousin was spoiled and too used to having her own way. They thought she was a bad influence on their daughter and cut the vacation short.

As they got into the taxi back at the airport, Abby said predictably, "Oh no, not another taxi. We—"

To their surprise, this time Jeannie cut her off. "Oh, Abby, stop acting like a brat."

The parents, who had worried that Jeannie was starting to imitate Abby, sighed in relief. They were surprised again when they returned to New York and Abby told her parents that taxis were okay and they should try one sometime.

Should you avoid traveling with someone else's kids just because they're used to a more luxurious lifestyle than your budget can deliver? According to Sandra Hatch, a Los Angeles–based psychotherapist, that depends on the personality of the child. "Children with an open spirit for new experiences can adapt quickly, particularly if they know your expectations."

While you shouldn't automatically assume, then, that little Lord Fauntleroy won't enjoy your camping trip, you should tell him what to anticipate so he won't demand silk sheets for his sleeping bag.

What If the Kids Get Sick or Have an Accident?

Most parents understand that sickness or accidents can happen any time, and as long as you act responsibly, they won't hold it against you if their child gets sick or has an accident while in your care. But if you're the type who goes to pieces in such circumstances, it's probably best that you don't invite someone else's children on your vacation. If you do, however, don't burden yourself with constant anxiety over the possible but improbable.

One way to instill confidence that your guests will be well taken care of is to know as much as possible about them before you travel.

KNOW BEFORE YOU GO

Before you travel with someone else's kids, here are some of the topics you should discuss with their parents.

Medical History

Parents often know their children's medical history by memory. If their kids have been vaccinated for chicken pox, they won't worry when the kids are exposed to it. Ask the parents of the children in your charge to give you a few brief notes on each child's medical history before you leave. That way, when little pink bumps appear on their bodies you won't scratch your head and mumble, "Let's see, did your mom say you had chicken pox or could these be insect bites?"

If a child has medical problems such as epilepsy or diabetes, you'll want special instructions for diet, medication and emergency care. In fact, some travelers obtain a medical release from the children's parents that includes the name of each child, birth date, possible medical complications and the telephone number of their doctor.

Be prepared if the problem is as common as nearsightedness. Carry a copy of the child's lens prescription or be sure the child has an extra pair of glasses so you won't all have to sit in the first row at the movies.

Allergies

In the event of sickness or accident, you need to know if the child is allergic to penicillin or other medications, particularly if you can't reach the parents. Food allergies can be a problem too. An eight-year-old boy who was severely allergic to chocolate ended up in an emergency room when he ate a candy bar on a trip with his aunt and uncle. His parents didn't tell the relatives about the allergy because they figured their son knew to stay away from chocolate without prompting.

"Why didn't you tell us you were allergic to chocolate?" his uncle asked the boy.

"The doctor said I could outgrow it," he explained. "I grew an inch last month so I thought I had outgrown it. I guess I still have more growing to do."

Because you can't always rely on children to speak up concerning their own welfare, particularly if they're shy or afraid to be different, be sure to discuss allergies with their parents.

Foods They Like and Dislike

In a society of diverse ethnic backgrounds and regional influences, you can't assume that all kids like the same foods. Growing up on such Italian cold cuts as salami, prosciutto and capocolla, I winced the first time someone placed a ham sandwich in front of me. As for salad, why would anyone put curdled milk on lettuce (I had never seen Roquefort dressing before) instead of oil and vinegar? It turned my stomach.

Knowing in advance what foods your young guests like and dislike doesn't mean you have to cater to their every dining whim. However, if you don't want to bring them home to their parents several pounds lighter, be sure to include at least some food choices they recognize and like.

Normal Bed Time

If the youngsters you take to Florida are used to nine hours of sleep and your travel schedule allows only seven, don't be surprised if they would rather sleep in the car than tour Cape Canaveral.

Children who stay up past their normal bedtime can become cranky, sluggish, silent, sleepy or the opposite—hyperactive, loud or zany. But what's a vacation if it's no different from the norm? While an evening or two off their normal schedule may have little effect on them, a week or more of strange hours can alter attitude, behavior and physical stamina.

Movies They Can See

A couple took their kids and a seven-year-old neighbor on a weekend trip. To avoid sex and foul language on the screen, they took the group to a G-rated film about a heroic dog. When the girl told her parents about the film, they were upset. As animal-rights activists, they objected to the mistreatment of the dog by some characters in the film and, in fact, had picketed the movie in their hometown.

One way to avoid taking someone else's kids to a movie their parents disfavor is to discuss current movie offerings with the parents before you travel, or at least what rating standards (e.g., PG, PG-13) they normally apply.

Religious Observances

When you take on the responsibility of caring for someone else's kids, that includes their religious needs as well. Don't assume that just because your family prefers to sleep in on Sunday that your guests do too. Some children are too shy to tell you they would like to go to church or temple but carry a heavy conscience if they don't. If your vacation will take you to a location where their church or other place of worship is inaccessible, be sure to make that known in advance so the kids and their parents can decide on an alternative. Don't forget to ask about dietary observances as well.

Checklist

Unless you're a whiz kid yourself, how can you remember all the details about someone else's kids? You don't have to. Give their parents a checklist or information form to fill out that you can carry with you. It could be as simple as this:

Name:	Little Miss Muffet
Medical History:	Has had chicken pox. Frequent ear infections. Needs glasses at the movies.
Allergies:	Strawberries
Favorite Foods:	Hamburgers, fries, pepperoni pizza, chicken, tacos
Doesn't Eat:	Lamb, sushi, peas, asparagus, brussels sprouts
Normal Bedtime:	8:30–9 P.M. Up at 7 A.M.
Movies:	G. Some PG.
Religious Observances:	Grace before meals

Limiting Logistical Problems

The Wallaces invited two of their children's school chums to fly with them to Phoenix, Arizona. They remembered to upgrade their usual mid-size rental car to a full-size vehicle that would seat six. They forgot, however, to think about trunk space, and the kids in the backseat rode piggyback on the three suitcases to the hotel.

Fortunately, to keep logistical problems to a minimum, they had chosen a self-contained resort with endless activities. With three restaurants on the resort premises, the Wallaces had never needed reservations on previous stays. Tables for six, however, proved less prevalent than tables for four, and by the time their table was ready 90 minutes after they gave their name to the hostess at the Mexican restaurant, they were too full of tortilla chips and salsa to eat dinner.

A similar situation developed when they went to the movies. Although on time, they were too late to find six seats together.

You can adjust to many logistical problems that crop up when traveling with a larger number of people by remembering to make reservations or by arriving before everyone else. The Wallaces adjusted by dining the following night at a Chinese restaurant where larger tables were the rule. Another way to adjust is to face the reality that you may not always be together. As Mrs. Wallace told her husband, "We brought the other kids along so they could be together. We don't always have to be a party of six, even if we don't get the egg roll."

METHODOLOGY

Assigning Responsibilities

Just as you can assign responsibilities to your own kids when traveling, you can assign tasks to their friends as well. In fact, if they know their assigned tasks in advance, they can be very resourceful. On a summer vacation at a lake, a teenage guest was put in charge of locking up the fishing equipment when not in use. Since he had not fished much, he read up on the proper maintenance of rods and other tackle and taught the whole family how to care for them properly. While you needn't feel compelled to assign responsibilities if there aren't enough to go around, neither should you hesitate just because your kids' friends are guests. After all, assigning chores is one way to make your guests feel right at home.

Setting Ground Rules

A 12-year-old boy was the guest of his friend's family at a

resort. When he began clowning in the hotel pool, his friends did not follow suit because they knew their parents would get angry. Several other kids in the pool, however, began to imitate him, jumping topsy-turvy off the suspended bridge to see who could make the most remarkable splash. When his host noticed what was going on, he yelled at his preteen guest, who became embarrassed and remained quiet the rest of the trip.

While your own kids probably know what behavior they can get away with, it's unfair to expect clairvoyance from a child who doesn't know you as well. You can't anticipate every peccadillo youngsters might precipitate, but you can set ground rules for anticipated activities such as swimming and diving.

Sometimes kids will behave better in your presence because they don't want to be disciplined in front of their peers, thereby losing esteem. Particularly as children approach the age when their self-esteem hinges more heavily on acceptance by peers, you'll want to be sensitive to the potential embarrassment of your own children and their guests. It's a good idea not only to set ground rules so they know what's expected, but to give them fair warning by taking them quietly aside before you single them out publicly for improper behavior.

Exercising Authority

However you exercise authority with your own kids, whether by positive reinforcement ("Emmy, you were a perfect little lady at dinner") or by negative threats ("No allowance if you don't eat your peas"), you may question how much authority you can and should exercise over someone else's kids.

A West Coast couple invited their two East Coast nephews, ages 17 and 18, to meet them in Aspen for a ski vacation. Since the boys were much better skiers than the couple, they skied their separate ways and agreed to meet back at the rented condo at 3:30 P.M. When the boys failed to show up by 5 P.M., the uncle phoned the ski patrol and started looking for the teens around town. The boys were found drinking beer in an après-ski bar where they had shown false I.D. cards.

The uncle told them he was going to call their dad and tell him they had been drinking.

"Oh, Dad won't mind. He lets us drink beer all the time," the boys responded.

At the risk of losing his nephews' affection, the uncle told the boys that while they were his responsibility they would have to abide by his rules or go home. Fortunately, the boys caught the seriousness of his tone and obliged.

Smaller children may not understand so readily why your expectations differ from their parents'.

A couple took their five-year-old niece on a weekend trip to visit other relatives. When the girl, ignoring all verbal admonitions, continued to race around the house with her younger cousins, her aunt spanked her.

Mortified, the girl bawled for hours and wanted to go home. Puzzled by what they considered an overreaction to a spanking, the couple called the girl's parents, who explained that their daughter had never been spanked because they didn't believe in corporal punishment. "But don't worry about it," her parents added. "She needs to learn that people are different and have different ways of handling things. I'm sure it was a good lesson for her."

Even if you could guess how someone else's parents would handle the same situation, their philosophy of discipline may not be yours. You can only exercise authority the way *you* think best, and if your guest can't adapt, chances are you'll both elect not to travel together again.

On the other hand, if you know your methods of exercising

authority are poles apart from the other parents', you may want to postpone travel together, at least until their children have had the opportunity to experience other authority figures such as teachers and coaches or are mature enough to adapt to new operating conditions.

Two against One—When Kids Take Sides

"Mommy, Michael and Tom are hogging the TV and won't let me watch any of my programs."

Whether it's television, movies, games or just conversation, it's not unusual for two or more children to occasionally take sides against a third friend or sibling. And it's not necessarily age that determines the balance of power.

An 8-year-old boy invited his pal to join his parents and 11-year-old sister on a trip to Zion National Park. Normally, brother and sister traveled well together, but when the friend discovered the sister hated bugs, both boys joined forces in tormenting her with spiders and beetles.

Parents or guardians should be cognizant of new alliances forged between their children and their guests at the expense of another child and intervene, when necessary, to keep the kids from "bugging" each other.

Guiding Social Behavior

What do you do when your travel guests demonstrate poor manners or a lack of social skills?

When you invite someone else's kids to join you on a trip, you are accepting them as they are, good and bad habits included. Habits that bother you may not bother everyone. Continually picking on the habits that irritate you can make a child feel inferior or defensive. And their parents may resent your unsolicited corrections as a negative commentary on their parenting abilities.

Do you keep silent, then, when Sally Ann loudly slurps the last drop of malt with her straw or Ricky inhales pasta from his plate like a paper shredder?

"Yes, you keep quiet," says one mother, who has traveled with other peoples' kids, ages 5 to 15. "You have no right to appoint yourself their teacher. Occasionally, however, you may have to guide them gracefully."

Her family, for example, was traveling with a 10-year-old boy who was in the habit of kicking off his shoes at restaurants and slouching in the chair. "At a McDonald's it didn't matter, but I took him aside before we went to a four-star restaurant and said, 'Johnny, this is a very proper restaurant we are going to and they don't like it when people lounge in their seats or take their shoes off, so tonight we'll have to ask you to sit up and keep your shoes on.' And he did.

"Usually when asked in a diplomatic way, a child will do his best to cooperate. If not, he won't be our guest again."

Another way to guide social behavior without hurting someone's feelings is by example. Hopefully, if a kid sees he's the only one licking the ice cream off his plate, he'll stop doing it. Or at least wait until no one's looking.

Looking Out for Each Other

A couple traveled with six children, three of their own plus three friends, ranging in age from 5 to 12.

"At first we went crazy keeping track of them and responding to each one's needs of the moment. Finally, we took advantage of the natural resources under our noses and teamed each older kid with a younger one. This proved particularly helpful at places like zoos and amusement parks, where eight pairs of eyes were needed to watch everyone."

The older kids escorted the younger ones to the restroom, helped them through the chow line, and held the money and tickets for their rides.

"Teaming teaches the older kids to take responsibility for someone else and prevents them from ignoring the younger ones. The kids cooperate because they know if we get too tired, we won't want to invite their friends again for a long, long time.

"The truth is, however, that now we wouldn't dream of traveling with our kids unless we had someone else's along to help."

Who Pays What?

When you invite someone else's kids on a trip, be clear about which expenses you are willing to cover.

For example, if you intend to pay for everything, you might say to the child's parents, "Harold and I would like to invite Julie to join us in Hawaii. We'll pay for her plane ticket and all other expenses if you let her come."

If you're willing to cover only a portion of the additional expenses, you could say, "Julie said she'd love to go to Hawaii with us. If you buy her airplane ticket, she can stay free in our condo. There's plenty of room and I don't think she would need more than $250 to cover meals and other expenses."

Or, if your guest's parents are expected to pay all costs, be specific: "If Julie wants to join us on our Globetrotter Tour of Hawaii, the rate per person is $1,500 including airfare, hotels, sightseeing and meals. If she can come, you can just call in your credit card number to the travel agency."

By the way, if one or more of your guests are paying for their own meals, it's easier to keep an expense log and settle the bills later, rather than collecting money at every meal. While this method may not be as exact, it's less cumbersome, and if you are going to worry about recouping every penny, it's probably best not to invite guests at all.

Whatever method you choose, be sure it's absolutely clear. Don't rely on telephone conversations because people often forget what they've agreed to verbally, especially if changes are made along the way. After you and the parents have agreed on who pays what and when payments will be made, follow up with a note.

Dear John and Martha,

We are delighted that Matthew will be joining us on our trip to Yellowstone. Here's the invoice from the travel agency for his plane ticket and share of the hotel room costs. Note that the ticket is completely nonrefundable, so you may want to take out cancellation insurance.

As we discussed, you can give us $200 to cover his meals and other expenses, and we'll return any money left over or absorb any costs above that amount.

Oh, I forgot to remind Matthew that he'll need boots, as we plan to do some hiking.

This way neither set of parents will have to shell out for items they never intended to pay for.

Follow Up

As with any trip, when you travel with someone else's kids, you learn what places and activities were enjoyed most or least, what you would do the same or differently and what problems you would try to avoid next time. But when you try to recall these thoughts a year later, your memory may be as dim as the lighting in some hotel rooms.

"What's the name of that charming restaurant in Santa Fe we loved?"

"That was in Albuquerque, darling."

"No sweetheart, we didn't stop in Albuquerque. We went right to Phoenix, remember?"

"I've never been to Phoenix."

Jot down whatever you wish to remember a year later, and pop the information into your trip file (the same one you used to keep tickets, confirmations or brochures when you started the trip). You can use the back of a postcard that identifies the place you visited, or type your comments on your personal computer. You don't have to write an essay, just a few notes that will jog your memory:

> The kids loved the Just Like Home Motel, which had a cookie jar in every room. Jody's friend was a perfect little guest but cried because she forgot her bathing suit. Next time, bring an extra just in case.
>
> The Round-Up Ranch was great. Room 22 has the perfect location, next to the ice cream machine.

Don't forget to evaluate whether you would invite the same kids, or any kids, in the future.

Finally, if you enjoyed your young guests, take the time to tell them and their parents, not just when parting company, but later— when the special effort of a written note will signal your sincerity. It's one more opportunity to make someone else's kids feel special.

How to Travel with Parents, In-Laws and Other Relatives

Advantages

Rick, an attorney client, called me one winter to plan a trip to Hawaii for himself, his wife and five-year-old child; his brother, sister-in-law and their baby; and his mother. Rick and his family were having trouble selecting a place to stay.

His mother wanted to stay at the same deluxe hotel on Maui that she and her late husband had frequented. It had special meaning for her and she felt comfortable there.

Rick, however, an avid golfer, wanted a hotel with a good golf plan. His wife didn't play golf, but she knew one thing: No way was she going to cook breakfast or it wouldn't be a vacation.

Rick's brother, on the other hand, saw no reason to spend $30 or $40 for breakfast at a hotel, particularly with a nine-month-old. He preferred to stay in a condominium, which would not only have a kitchen but a washer and dryer as well. His wife liked the idea that the condo also provided daily maid service.

The families resolved their dilemma by agreeing to fly together to Maui, where Rick's mother checked into her favorite hotel. Rick's brother checked into a one-bedroom condominium that was adjacent to his mother's hotel, while Rick and his family checked into a nearby hotel with a top-rated golf course. Every day they met on the beach in front of his mother's hotel so she wouldn't have to walk too far. When they felt like it, they would go their separate ways, usually getting together for dinner.

It might have been easier for these relatives to plan separate trips, but they would have missed sharing time together.

The main advantage of traveling with parents, in-laws and other relatives is the opportunity to bring an extended family closer together. In a relaxed atmosphere free from the usual daily hassles, relatives can enjoy each other's best moods and develop positive feelings about each other.

It's also an opportunity for grandchildren to share time with grandparents while the latter are still physically fit enough to travel. Twenty years hence, they'll still remember the time the family went to Lake Michigan and Grandpa slipped fish on their hooks when they weren't looking. Particularly if the grandparents live far away, the few days or weeks spent together on a vacation may be the most special time grandchildren will share with their grandparents.

Since most people enjoy travel, some use it as an opportunity to do something special for their parents. Who hasn't bought a new car, enjoyed a theatrical performance or discovered a new restaurant and thought, "Mom and Pop would sure love this"? Inviting our parents on a vacation is one way to show them that we appreciate and care about them.

Disadvantages

Unless you're used to living with parents, in-laws or other relatives, you may miss your privacy when traveling with them—the privacy to keep the volume up on the television, raid the refrigerator in the buff at three in the morning or trade barbs with your spouse and kids. Just like travel with the boss or friends, you give up a degree of freedom to say or do what you please.

And just like traveling with friends or kids, there is more preparation involved when traveling with relatives and, if you are treating, more cost too. But the extra cost may pale next to your parents' financial sacrifices, the ones they made to give you piano lessons, straight teeth and a degree in ancient Kushite literature.

More time together can also mean more time to get on each other's nerves. If your rapport with your parents or in-laws is shaky to begin with, you risk deeper damage to the relationship.

A woman spent a weekend with her son and his wife in New Orleans. While shopping, she spotted a cookbook she had enjoyed and bought it for her daughter-in-law as a gift. To the wife, however, the gift implied that she didn't know how to cook. She became enraged and wouldn't talk to her mother-in-law the rest of the trip. The young couple had married without parental approval and there was still mistrust on both sides. It was a long time before the incident blew over.

Although sensitive relationships can rupture anytime, even at home, there is more opportunity when relatives spend a concentrated period of time together. Sometimes one relative will begin to feel relaxed and less guarded in what he or she says or does, while the other is still ultrasensitive, leading to misinterpretation of motives.

While they may want to develop a closer relationship, relatives who still have ambivalent feelings about each other should postpone shared travel until confident they'll get along together.

PLANNING CONSIDERATIONS

What Type of Travelers Are They?

A man called me to plan a trip to Hawaii with his wife and three small children. He said his mother- and father-in-law would be going too. Although the in-laws were comfort seekers who preferred to stay in the best hotels, they were willing to compromise slightly, or so they said, to join the kids. The son-in-law, whose family often spent weekends in the cramped quarters of a sailing boat, felt a two-bedroom condo would be ample space at a reasonable cost.

We tried to find a compromise property that would satisfy both parties, but it became evident that the parents didn't want to give up the services of a deluxe hotel and the son-in-law didn't want to pay for services he didn't need.

When the younger couple decided not to go at all, the in-laws were relieved. "Now can you book us into the hotel we wanted in the first place?" they asked.

No matter how close relatives may be at home, the fact that they're related does not necessarily make them compatible travelers. And even if one couple pays for the other's trip, it doesn't make their budgets compatible.

A son stopped inviting his dad along on his family's vacation because the father, having grown up during the Depression, was uncomfortable with and critical of his son's spending. When they stayed in luxury quarters, the father would scold, "A suite? Why do you need a suite? One room was good enough when you were growing up. How can you be so extravagant?"

"You're right, Dad, but we're going to order room service anyway."

The son now gifts his dad with "budget" tours he can take on his own and feel good about.

Who Pays What?

Before you travel with relatives, make clear which costs, if any, you intend to cover. Sometimes a problem develops when a relative who is better off financially insists on paying everyone else's expenses.

One son-in-law, Steven, earned a comfortable salary to support his family, but nothing to match the millions his father-in-law, J.J., had accumulated as president of a large banking firm. No matter what costs father- and son-in-law agreed to share before the families traveled together, the father-in-law insisted on picking up the tab for everything. When Steve checked out of a hotel, he was told the bill had already been taken care of—dinners, telephone calls and personal items included.

Steven didn't like feeling obligated to his in-laws nor subjected to J.J.'s tendency to dictate where they should go, where they should dine, and what they should do. Steve resented his father-in-law's "taking control" of their vacation as if he were chairman of the board.

One way to keep your bill all to yourself is to prepay not only the room rate with tax but also enough to cover meals, drinks and extras at the hotel. As long as you are dealing with a reputable hotel or travel agent, there should be no problem getting refunds of overpayments, although refunds may take a few weeks for processing.

Another common conflict arises when a husband or wife wants to pay the way for a relative, but the other spouse is less than thrilled with the idea.

A wife wanted to reward her younger brother for completing his Ph.D. by inviting him to join herself and her husband on a trip to Hong Kong. Her husband agreed and they sent the brother an airline ticket. But as the trip progressed and the husband found himself paying for all the meals, tips and entertainment, he complained to his wife, "Your brother is such a mooch. He could offer to pay for something."

"But we invited him," his wife defended. "He doesn't have any money. He's just a poor student."

"That's what you've been saying for the last 15 years."

One way to foil flak from a spouse incensed at lavishing funds on *your* relative is to use your own money to pay for the relative. If you don't have your own cache of funds, buying a prepaid package with most expenses included will avoid opportunities for irritation every time you or your spouse dig into your pockets. Or treat the relative to a weekend trip, where the extra cost will be limited to a few days.

If, however, even a short trip will cause friction between you and your spouse, you can give your graduating relative a nice frame for his diploma instead.

Health Limitations

When I participated in a familiarization tour to Kenya a few years ago, one of the fellow travel agents on the trip was a grandmother who had lived with cancer for several years. Although her relatives at home didn't want her to go, she didn't miss an activity in our whirlwind schedule, whether it was bouncing in the back of a jeep on a three hour game run or climbing into a hot air balloon to float over the Masai Mara at dawn.

While a positive attitude can sometimes compensate for imperfect health, age often brings on limitations that can't be ignored. Before you plan travel with older relatives, be sure you allow for and *accept* these limitations. If you don't know the relative well, here are some common problems to consider before you plan the trip:

- *How much walking will be required?* A bad knee, hip or back can make long walks painful for some older persons, as can poor circulation.

- *What is the altitude at your destination?* If your guest has heart or breathing problems, you'll want to avoid high altitudes. It's best to consult with a doctor to determine which altitudes are safe for relatives with these problems.

- *How extreme will the weather be?* Will excessive rain, or dampness aggravate arthritis? Will intense heat or cold affect delicate health?

- *Will a range of foods be available?* This is a consideration if your guest is diabetic or has any other condition restricting diet.

- *Are doctors and hospitals readily accessible?* While this is a good question for anyone who travels, the odds for medical problems obviously increase with age.

Once you're aware of any health limitations, be sure that everyone in your party can live with them so you won't hear your kids groan when Grandpa says, "I can't walk any farther. Let's go home."

Travel Insurance

Since many airline tickets, tours, cruises and hotels have cancellation penalties, in some cases as much as 100 percent of the cost, you'll want to consider trip cancellation insurance particularly when older relatives will be traveling in your group. If your trip costs thousands of dollars, insurance premiums can be a considerable expense. Compare the cancellation policies of tour operators, cruise lines and hotels. If all other aspects of the trip are equal, you may want to take the line with the most liberal refund policy.

Evacuation insurance is another type of coverage you may want to consider to reimburse costs of transporting the ill in an emergency or their remains. While you may prefer not to think about the possibility of someone dying en route, the shock of death can be compounded by the shock of costs for shipping the body home from Perth, Australia.

Activities for Everyone

A client in her 60s called me to arrange a ski trip to Keystone, Colorado, with three other women. They wanted lodging close to the lifts because one of the ladies was 84 and didn't like to carry her skis too far.

It's inspiring to know that age alone does not dictate when we sell our luggage at a garage sale and donate our ski boots to the Museum of Early American Folklore. But just as parents can be over-protective of children, children can grow up to be overprotective of their senior citizen parents, relegating them to reading or knitting by the fire in the lodge.

While it would be a mistake to exclude an elderly relative from river rafting, horseback riding or any other activity merely because of age, neither should you assume that parents still enjoy the same interests and activities they once did. People's idea of fun can change over the years, and even if the spirit is willing, sometimes the flesh flounders.

A couple was invited to spend a week with their son and his family at their isolated mountain cabin. When the younger family members took the car each day to a local ski resort, the grandparents were left without transportation to the nearest town, which was five miles away. Icy walkways made even short walks precarious, and after two days of staying in all day, the couple was bored as stiff as the joints in their knees.

Another couple took the wife's mother along to a hotel on Miami Beach. The husband and wife were tired from working and looked forward to doing nothing but napping or reading by the pool. The mother, however, who spent most of her days relaxing around the pool at her condo was ready to "go, go, go." And that's just what she did, taking one-day tours to the Everglades, West Palm Beach and Key West. When she wasn't touring, she took a cab or the monorail to go shopping. Fortunately, Miami was a place where she could get around easily.

Before you take relatives who no longer ski to a ski resort, or who no longer swim to the beach, investigate the availability of other activities in the area such as going to the movies, to museums, shopping or sightseeing. Most importantly, be sure there's a way for them to get where they want to go.

Assigning Responsibilities

Just as you might assign your children responsibilities they can handle when traveling, don't overlook your parents and in-laws for certain tasks. Sometimes, the less we expect from an older relative, the less they feel they can do. You wouldn't ask your 80-year-old father to change a flat tire as long as you could do it, but you can probably think of a few tasks that would make elderly relatives feel needed and useful. Here are a few.

Before the trip:

1. Research restaurants or sights at your destination.

2. Check on visa or immunization requirements.

3. Check the weather forecasts in areas you'll be driving through.

4. Check on baggage restrictions.

5. Learn some basic vocabulary in the language of any foreign countries you will visit.

6. Learn how to count to 20 in that language.

During the trip:

1. Keep the trip diary or expense log.

2. Become familiar with local currency exchange rates.

3. Find out how to place a call from a public telephone in each foreign country you will visit.

4. Recheck flight departure times as you go along.

5. Check on the departure times of shuttle buses to the airport and the length of time needed to get there.

But don't invite your relatives along just to babysit your kids at the hotel while you climb Pike's Peak. There's a difference between making them feel useful and making them feel used.

PITFALLS TO AVOID

Friendly Advice or Interference

"The problem with traveling with my mother," says a friend of mine, "is that she never stops being my mother. It doesn't matter that I'm 40 years old. When I visit her at home, she behaves more like a friend because she hasn't seen me for a few weeks. But when we travel together, she gets back to being Mom in a flash, telling me how I should dress and manage my children."

As the saying goes, once a parent, always a parent. And all parents have opinions formed by feelings of responsibility for offspring, no matter how old they are. This natural inclination of parents to jump headlong into the lives of their grown children may result from a keen interest in their welfare but can be perceived as nothing more than a nosy annoyance.

The difference between the two is often in the ear of the listener. The same parental *advice* that a son or daughter is used to accepting or ignoring becomes *interference* when it comes from a mother- or father-in-law.

For relatives who have to weigh each word and can't be themselves, a trip with their grown children won't be much of a vacation. Parents who can't adjust to the fact that their children are adults won't be comfortable traveling with children who can't adjust to parents who still act like parents.

Taking Sides

Riddle: Why do grandchildren get along so well with their grandparents? Answer: Because they both have the same enemy—the parents.

Free from the responsibilities of parenting, some grandparents can lavish their love unconditionally on their grandchildren. The grandchildren, in turn, can respond to love that imposes no conditions and is a reliable font of candy and cookies. This easy relationship is one to be savored and doesn't usually become a problem unless it undermines the authority of the parents.

Three generations of McMillans rented a beach house for a month vacation in Bar Harbor, Maine. When the teenage son failed to return his parents' car in time for his sister to use on an outing with her friends, the boy's parents took away his driving privileges for the duration of their stay.

"But I'm suppose to take my new friends to the party at the Lee's tomorrow night," he pleaded.

"Not until you learn to be more responsible," his father insisted.

"Yeah," chimed in his sister.

The next day, Grandpa McMillan took the side of the boy and told him, "You can use my car if you promise to bring it back on time."

The boy's father was upset with his own father for damaging his authority as a parent.

"You're not the boss of this family," his son chastised him.

"I was just trying to help him out," the grandfather defended. "Don't you remember when you were 17 and stayed out so late with Maryjo that your mother and I missed our flight to Cleveland?"

"Sure I remember," the father answered, "I remember catching hell from you, remember?"

At times, a grandparent's interference can help mend strained family ties and create a bridge between alienated relatives. And sometimes, interference can be a nuisance, plain and simple. When and how to apply the unique influence of a grandparent is an art often learned by trial and error.

If, however, grandparents find themselves continually at odds with the parents over the grandchildren, they could be overstepping their role, a perception that will likely be reinforced if the family travels together.

Likewise, relatives who take sides in a disagreement between a husband and wife can find themselves in a no-win situation. If they side with their blood relation, the other spouse will discount their opinion as biased. And if they side with the in-law instead of their son, daughter, sister, cousin, etc., they may be accused of disloyalty.

A woman joined her sister and brother-in-law on a cruise. After a few days at sea, the wife had a tiff with her husband over what she considered his flirtatious behavior with another passenger at their table.

Alone with her sister, the wife called her husband every name imaginable. Her sister agreed and added, "Do you know what he said about you? He said you were an immature dummy."

A few days later, however, when the couple had made up, the sister was perceived as a "snitch" by the brother-in-law and "interfering" by his wife. Fed up with both of them, the sister found companionship with the single officers at the captain's table and resolved to travel alone on the next cruise.

"We Vacationed with Your Mother Last Year"

I have a client, a husband and father of four, who calls every year for information and brochures on some exotic destination like Katmandu or Machu Pichu. But instead of going to these places, every summer he and the family return once again to Sicily to visit his wife's mother.

"Do you think I will ever convince my wife to go somewhere besides Sicily?" he complains. "At this rate I'll never see anything else."

His wife, on the other hand, says, "Sure, his folks live close by. We see them all the time, but we see my parents only once a year. Who knows how much longer they'll be around? If we went somewhere else, I'd feel guilty and wouldn't enjoy the trip anyway."

For this couple, it wasn't a matter of limited vacation time but of limited funds. Transporting a family of six is like having Pac-Man living in your wallet, gobbling up your money. Few families can afford the experience more than once a year.

Individuals whose parents or relatives live far away face this dilemma year after year. If a spouse seeks to break the pattern, the inevitable argument arises: "We visited your mother last year. Now it's time to visit my dad," or "Why can't we go to Europe next year instead of visiting your mother?"

Inviting relatives to visit you doesn't solve the problem if you use your vacation time to show them around. But there are a couple of ways to break out of this vacation mold if you find it too limiting.

The first is to cut your time with the relatives in half and use the rest of the time to go somewhere else en route. If you visit your relatives first, you may find it difficult to break away when everyone is begging you to stay until Uncle Tio's wedding or Joey's oboe recital. It's easier for them to accept the "I have to be back at work on Monday" explanation. For example, my client who always visits Sicily has convinced his wife to fly first to Athens for a one-week Greek island cruise before spending the second week with the in-laws.

A second alternative takes a great deal more organization and planning. It's a family reunion at a different destination each year. This way you can see the relatives and experience a new place at the same time. Your choices would be limited to destinations that are accessible to everyone's budget and physical abilities, but hopefully these places will be more interesting than the annual trek to Poughkeepsie.

If travel to the destination you're dying to visit is too expensive to combine with a visit to the relatives, you would be better off alternating years: one year you visit Grandpa in Dubuque, and the next you visit King Tut's tomb. After all, while no one knows how long the old folks will be around, neither do you know how long you'll be around to make that dream trip to the Giluwe Valley of New Guinea.

Comparisons

"We spent more on your mother last year," a wife told her husband in my office when he balked at the cost of the cruise she had booked for themselves and her parents.

"But my mother is used to the best," the husband explained. "Your parents are used to traveling in a camper. Let's give them a cheaper cabin on the lowest deck."

"But then our cabin will be better than theirs," the wife rebutted.

"So what?" her husband shrugged.

Some people who enjoy taking good care of their own parents on a trip develop a blasé attitude when traveling with in-laws.

If you find yourself applying different standards for your in-laws than your relatives, examine your motives. Do the in-laws prefer traveling in a more casual, less expensive mode, or are you just discriminating against them, consciously or subconsciously?

While you examine the reasons for any considerable differences in trip expenditures, avoid becoming a nitpicker: "We took your parents on a 10-day cruise. Why are we taking mine on a 7-day cruise?" Chronic comparisons like this can inhibit experimentation and spontaneity and take the joy out of traveling with relatives.

Sibling Rivalry at the Age of 40

A friend told me a story about the time she and her husband, Larry, flew to Cabo San Lucas, Mexico, with Larry's sister, Gloria, and her husband, Dave.

> No sooner had we settled in our adjacent rooms in Cabo when Larry and his sister both became 40ish going on 4. Gloria saw our room and exclaimed, "Oh, you just have a pool view. We have a great view of the ocean from our room."
>
> After checking his sister's room, Larry wanted to know why we didn't have an ocean view because I had made the reservations.
>
> "Luck of the draw," I explained. "We asked for adjacent rooms and they got the one in the corner."
>
> Larry wouldn't rest until he got a room just like his sister's down the hall. The room he finally settled on was smaller than our previous room, but now the view matched hers.
>
> When we piled into the rental car for the ride to the fishing boat, Dave and Gloria were already in the front seat. Larry wanted them to move to the back because he gets carsick in the

backseat. But Gloria wouldn't move, not even after Larry reminded her of the cross-country trip they took when they were kids and how he got sick in the backseat and threw up on her. Fortunately, Dave was gracious enough to let Larry drive while he moved to the backseat and spared us all from déjà vu.

The fishing went fine for several hours. We had all caught enough dorado to feed the town. Then Gloria bagged a seven-foot sailfish and Larry turned green—but not from seasickness.

While Dave and Gloria relaxed the following day, Larry insisted on another eight hours of fishing so he could get a sail-fish bigger than Gloria's. He didn't. But I did and he was the first to tell Gloria about it. She said that was nice, but it was too bad we missed the film crew that was at the hotel in the afternoon making a motion picture. They got to meet all the stars and were asked to be extras in the movie.

Larry's face fell. "Well, that will make it a B movie for sure," Larry told her.

Finally I said, "If you two will stop this one-upmanship, we'll all have a better time."

"You're right," Larry said. "It's just a habit."

Then Dave mentioned that he and Gloria had just received their Broncos tickets for the season. They were a little off to the side, on the 20-yard line.

"We got great seats," Larry told him, "dead center on the 50-yard—"

He didn't get a chance to finish. All three of us got up and left the table. We came back, but Larry got the message. And the rest of the trip went fine.

The message for Larry and others like him is that it's more comfortable for everyone when relatives aren't rivals, but instead play on the same team (or, "don't begrudge unto others lest they begrudge unto you").

No Mother-in-Law Jokes, Please

At the airport, I overheard a man checking in for a party of three at the airline counter.

"Smoking or nonsmoking?" the ticket agent asked.

"Put my wife and me in nonsmoking and my mother-in-law out on the wing somewhere," he laughed.

The ticket agent smiled, "Seriously, shall I put her across the aisle or in the row behind you?"

"Oh, put her behind me. Then I won't have to look at her."

"Come on," the ticket agent laughed, "she can't be that bad."

"You never met my mother-in-law," the passenger said. "She makes Bonzo look like Miss America."

A little later I saw this same man talking with his wife and the now infamous mother-in-law, an attractive woman with a congenial smile. I wondered if he had been testing out a new comedy routine on the airline agent or merely succumbing to the mother-in-law joke habit for an easy laugh.

Like Polish jokes, mother-in-law jokes may produce a chuckle, but also like Polish jokes, they tend to perpetuate untruths through mere repetition. So the next time you travel with your spouse's mother, leave the mother-in-law jokes to professional comedians.

Evaluation

When you travel with parents, in-laws and other relatives, it's useful to make a few notes to help in planning the next trip together, particularly if you experienced problems along the way. Keep in mind that one or two years hence, the physical capabilities of elderly relatives are apt to diminish. A hotel with 50 steps to the beach may present no problem this year, but next year it might. If, on the other hand, this year's hotel offers easy access for the elderly, you can note that for the future when it may be important.

And don't forget, if you enjoyed the companionship of your parents or any other relatives, be sure to tell them. They like to hear nice comments as much as you do.

NINE

How to Survive Traveling by Yourself

Advantages

Lily, a friend's daughter, went to England for a year of study abroad. Afterward she traveled by herself through Europe. She had joined the International Youth Hostel Federation so she could save money on accommodations and meet other young people along the way.

One morning in Basil, Switzerland, she met another student, a young Irish fellow, at breakfast. They discovered they would both be going to Florence, Italy, that afternoon and agreed to take the same train. Six hours after leaving Switzerland, Lily asked the conductor in broken Italian when they would reach Florence. To her shock, she was told that the train had already passed Florence an hour earlier (train stops are rarely announced) and was just pulling in to Rimini on Italy's east coast.

The two students jumped off the train in Rimini, ran through the station and jumped onto a train facing the opposite direction. Luckily, it was headed to Florence. To Lily's dismay, she was the only female on a train jammed with hundreds of Italian construction workers. Soon they all seemed to be pushing closer and closer to get a look at her. Uneasy, she threw her arms around her new acquaintance and kissed him passionately.

"Just pretend we're married," she told the surprised student. For the first time on her trip, she was fearful of appearing to be a lone traveler and grateful that someone else was with her. The Irish fellow was equally delighted, and the two students continued to tour together the rest of the summer.

The principal advantage of traveling by yourself is the freedom to do what you want when you want. It's the freedom to meander for five hours through the Louvre peering at each painting or to race through in five minutes, just long enough to see the *Mona Lisa* and say you've been there. It's the freedom to sleep late one morning without a tour leader pounding on your door at 6 A.M. so you won't miss the bus to Versailles. It's the freedom to wile away an extra day or two on the beach at Nice because no one else must be back home on time. No one else's desires to consider. No one else to blame if mistakes are made. No one to blame you. "Playing it by ear" is a solo, not a symphonic, performance. The itinerary is determined only by *your* time, *your* budget, *your* personality.

And while people traveling together have each other and may be less inclined to seek companionship, a lone traveler tends to be more open to meeting others along the way, creating a greater opportunity for new experiences. It's easier to accept a dinner invitation if you don't have to leave a companion alone in a hotel room.

Other important benefits are the self-reliance and personal growth garnered when traveling alone. Reserved travelers may be required to become outgoing when managing on their own. Spontaneous travelers may learn to budget time and money or risk running out of both.

Disadvantages

Depending on the place, lone travelers may find limitations on their activities. For example, many of us are reluctant to walk the streets of some cities at night. It would be unwise to hike an isolated forest trail by yourself, no matter how good you feel physically. And while not dangerous, it would feel awkward to most of us to dance alone at a disco.

While we can enjoy our aloneness, some of us have a need that can be met only by the presence of another person, preferably someone we love. It's this need that prompts a husband to take his new wife to his hometown to see the neighborhood he grew up in. It's the reason we drag a lover or spouse to the quaint, memorable town in the Alps we've already visited, albeit with someone else. We want them to share the same experience, the same feelings we had, romantic, majestic or inspirational.

Whether being on your own is more of a boon than a bust depends on your point of view. While a student at Cambridge in England one summer, I had fun punting down the narrow Cam River that ran along the backs of the colleges. The arched bridges over the river joined meticulous gardens alive with red, yellow and orange tulips, peonies and roses. Weeping willows, their graceful branches brushing the water, gave the scene the look of a Constable painting. But I felt something was missing because I wasn't sharing the beauty with someone special. Other students from my university were also studying at Cambridge, including a young woman who was with her boyfriend. They did everything together, and I thought how lucky they were to be able to share the trip.

Several years later I ran into this woman and we reminisced about that summer. I told her how at the time I envied the fact that she had someone to share it with.

"Are you kidding?" she said. "I envied all of you. There you were, free to meet other guys and have adventures while I was stuck with my boyfriend because my parents wouldn't let me go alone. They trusted him more than they trusted me." Although she was happily married to the same boyfriend, that summer in Europe she would have preferred the freedom of traveling without him.

While many travelers enjoy traveling completely on their own, some prefer the company of others at least occasionally. A client flies alone to Hong Kong every year because she likes to shop without interference from anyone. When she tours an exotic new destination, however, she prefers to join a group for sightseeing and other activities.

TRAVEL THAT WILL MAXIMIZE CONTACT WITH OTHERS

Some solo travelers like to meet other people when they travel. Here are some ways to maximize contact with others when traveling alone.

Escorted Tours

The easiest way to ensure meeting other people is to join an escorted tour, which usually consists of a group of 10 to 40 people led by a professional tour guide. In this way, you have company when sightseeing, dining or traveling from country to country.

When traveling on a tour, you'll pay a supplement over the advertised per person rate for single occupancy of a room because per person rates are based on double occupancy (two people contributing to the cost of the room). This supplement can sometimes be eliminated if you are willing to "list for a share." You simply let the tour company know that you're willing to share your room and if another passenger of the same sex also lists for a share, you'll be put together. Some companies offer "guaranteed shares" whereby they guarantee you'll pay the double occupancy rate even if they don't find someone to share your room.

To avoid a single supplement of $395, a 43-year-old secretary from San Diego signed up for a share on a trip to Australia. The tour company matched her with a roommate of similar age, a radiologist from Grand Rapids, Michigan. The two women got along so well that they now plan their annual trips together, despite the geographical distance between them.

The key here is to know yourself. Are you generally tolerant of other people and their habits? Can people tolerate your habits? Do you snore, smoke, go to bed at 8 P.M., wake up at 5 A.M.? If you really love your solitude, you would be wise to pay the single supplements.

Although neither your travel agent nor the tour company can guarantee what the other people on a tour group will be like, you can make certain generalizations. If your tour originates in the United States, you can assume that most of the other tour members will be American or Canadian. If you prefer to see England with the English, however, you could choose a tour that originates in London. Generally, the more expensive, more deluxe and longer the tour, the older the group members. Conversely, the cheaper the tour, the younger the travelers.

In any group, you may find one or two obnoxious individuals—the ones who hold up the bus while they bargain the "witch doctor" down another dime for his recipe book of exotic brews or the chronic complainers who grumble that their room faces the muddy part of the river, they didn't get a fortune cookie with their chop suey or the chambermaid doesn't speak English.

If you're under 35, you may want to consider one of the tour groups like Contiki, Club Europa or AESU that specialize in tours for the 18 to 35 age group. If you're a student, numerous tour packages are available for students only. If you're over 50, Elderhostel sponsors trips geared to retirees and seniors.

If your primary purpose for traveling is to meet single members of the opposite sex, tours featuring more adventuresome destinations tend to attract more singles. Odds are, while you may not meet the "love of your life," you will make a few friends.

In addition to providing some security during your trip, an escorted tour provides other benefits. A good guide can tell you more about a place than you would read in a travel book. You don't have to carry your luggage or waste precious vacation time translating train and bus schedules, asking for directions or making other travel arrangements. These chores are all handled for you.

The trade-off is that, aside from a few "at leisure" hours in the itinerary, you have little freedom of choice. You have to be at breakfast at eight o'clock because the bus leaves at nine. If a handsome prince invites you to his castle in Bavaria, too bad because your tour is leaving for Zurich. And if you find a lovely antique desk in London that goes on sale next Wednesday, forget it. By that time, you'll be in Dublin.

Hosted Packages

If the regimentation of an escorted tour is an anathema to you, you may want to consider a "hosted" tour. When you purchase one of these, you fly on your own to the destination. You are met and transferred to the hotel that is reserved for you. But aside from one or two city tours where you join other tourists from other hotels, you're on your own and free to travel or dine however you wish. You can, in this way, retain a measure of freedom but still join a group for a side trip or nightclub tour when you want the company of others or the services of a guide.

Cruises

Cruising is another way to be with people when traveling alone. Since you will dine at the same table each evening with four to seven other strangers, you are guaranteed to meet a few people. Do not, however, expect to find a "love boat" atmosphere.

Most cruises are populated by couples, families or retired persons. The latter group is attracted to cruising because it provides a vacation free from the hassle of lugging luggage, checking in and out of hotels, and getting on and off of trains, planes and other conveyances. Cruising does not require strenuous activity and many people, women in particular, feel safer at sea than they would by themselves in a hotel room in a major city. Women on their own who love to dance often choose a ship line that employs "hosts" as dance partners.

An older single man can be in great demand on a cruise. My uncle, a widower, took his first cruise at the age of 70. At dinner, he was seated with seven single ladies who kept him busy not only during but also after the cruise. Since then, cruising has become his favorite way of traveling.

A young woman in her 20s or 30s, however, should not select a cruise vacation with the idea that she'll meet her knight in shining armor. Most younger men are apt to take a girlfriend along. The situation is changing, however, as some cruise lines are now marketing to younger men and women by featuring a "party cruise" atmosphere.

The shorter three- and four-day cruises do attract more singles. And why not? The festive and romantic atmosphere on a ship can accelerate the pace of a new romance, already fueled by the knowledge that only a day or two remain to catalyze the romance before the trip ends. Where else can you devote all your attention to romance, whether swimming in the morning or dancing into the wee hours? Where else is someone captive to your pursuit, with no escape for three or four days? On the down side, it is difficult to avoid someone you would rather not see. Unless you lock yourself in your cabin all day, you're apt to run into each other.

A single executive in his early 50s told me about his difficulty escaping an aggressive middle-aged widow who hounded him from the first day of sailing. No matter where he went on the ship, there she was at his elbow. Before he could sneak into port when they docked in St. Thomas, she was already knocking on his cabin door, asking if they could go ashore together. If he went up to the gym to work out, she would don a leotard and try to keep up with the aerobics class. "When she persuaded the maître d' to change her table assignment to mine, I got desperate," he said. "I ate the rest of my dinners in my cabin and came out only when the coast was clear." The next time he went cruising, we put him on a 70,000-ton megaship with 10 decks, 2,500 passengers, 14 public rooms, 4 restaurants and less chance of running into the same person by chance.

In sum, if you're alone, cruising offers one more way to travel with people. But if your primary reason to travel is for romance, you may be disappointed. Check with your travel agent for advice on the cruise line that will most likely meet your expectations.

The All-Inclusive Concept

If ships make you seasick and you like sports, you may enjoy an all-inclusive resort that allows you the opportunity to be aloof but is also conducive to meeting others. Most of these resorts follow a concept popularized by a French company, Club Mediterranee (AKA Club Med), which developed resorts in more than 100 locations worldwide, including the United States, Mexico, Tahiti and the Caribbean.

The basic concept is that one price includes all: airfare, accommodations, meals, entertainment and instruction in numerous sports from windsurfing to skiing, depending on the location. Dining is family style so there's always a group of people to talk with at dinner if you choose. If you don't bring along your own roommate, the resort will provide one of the same sex. Numerous group activities encourage people to mix. Your travel agent can advise you on which all-inclusives tend to attract more singles and couples and which ones attract more families because of their children's programs.

Sports and Hobbies

A fifth-grade teacher asked me for trip suggestions six months before her summer vacation. She was 35 and single, and opportunities to meet single men in her work environment were as rare as a lottery jackpot. Where could she go, she wanted to know, to meet eligible men?

I told her while no tour operator, cruise line, resort or travel agent—myself included—could promise her "eligible men," I knew a few ways to increase the odds. "Do you participate in any sports?" I asked.

"I used to ski until I twisted my knee. I used to jog until I pulled a muscle in my thigh, and I used to ride horses until I moved to the city."

"What about golf?" I asked. Golf would not aggravate her knee or pulled muscle, and most cities have golf courses.

Although golf had never interested her, she decided to take a few lessons at a golf resort.

When she called a few months later, I asked how she was doing with her new sport. She reported that after a few lessons, her golf instructor had teamed her with a few of his other students, including a single lawyer. They had fallen in love and now she wanted to plan a honeymoon for two at another golf resort.

While many solo travelers have no interest in romance, few are natural hermits—most enjoy some social contact with others. Meeting people when you travel is one thing. Meeting people you have something in common with is another. One way to narrow the field is to plan a vacation that emphasizes a sport, hobby or seminar that interests you.

Your first step is to make a list of your interests and then have your travel agent match them to a group tour that includes those interests. For example, if you're an attorney who would like to learn to ski, you could investigate seminars designed for lawyers and held at ski resorts. In this way, you could increase your professional knowledge, meet others in your field, learn to ski and maybe even write off a portion of the trip expenses on your taxes. If you like to play tennis, you could spend a week at a tennis clinic where you would be matched with partners of similar ability.

Tours or packages are available for almost every leisure interest: scuba diving, fishing, golf, surfing, hiking, river rafting, chess, bridge, bird watching and horticultural tours to name just a few. If your interests are more intellectual, there are classical music tours and art gallery tours.

A company called Earthwatch, for example, packages tours devoted to conservation and scientific studies, but you don't have to be a scientist to go along. These trips have included excavating medieval castles in England, monitoring black rhinos in Zimbabwe, surveying life in Australia's rain forest canopy and helping to save endangered sea turtles in St. Croix.

Study and Travel

Juanita, a Mexican American from Albuquerque, was married to an Italian American who lamented that her pasta didn't taste like his mother's. Since her husband didn't have time to travel, Juanita enrolled in a class at a cooking school in Florence, Italy, a place she had always longed to see.

After several days of cooking classes, Juanita whipped up some fajitas, tortillas and chile rellenos at the request of her classmates. The instructor was so impressed, he convinced the school to offer a two-week course in the cuisine of the American Southwest and invited Juanita to teach it the following year.

She arrived home excited about the prospect of returning to Italy and began to perfect her favorite Mexican-American dishes. When her husband complained that he still wasn't getting pasta like Mama's, Juanita suggested that *he* sign up for a cooking class in Italy. He did and went with her to Florence the following summer.

Each year, thousands of high school and college age students travel to other parts of the world to study. But you don't have to be enrolled in school to combine study with travel. What you need is the *time* that coincides with the duration of the course you choose.

Ask yourself these questions: Do I like to study? and Am I willing to devote part of my vacation time to a class? If you answer yes to both questions, the next step is to find a class that appeals to you in a place you wish to visit.

A client who wanted to see France hesitated to go because he didn't speak the language. But what better time to learn a little French than on a two-week vacation among native speakers? Finding a language class can be as simple as reading the local newspaper ads from the city you wish to visit or reading international papers such as the European edition of the *Herald Tribune.* In this case, my client found a combination language study/travel tour offered through the extension program at a local university.

It's also possible to find subjects taught in English in foreign places. Five-day cooking classes, for example, are offered in English each summer at the Gritti Palace hotel in Venice, Italy.

You can start by listing topics that appeal to you. For example, if you're a culturist and your destination is Italy, your list might look like this:

- Italian language
- Art history
- Opera appreciation
- Ceramics
- Italian regional cooking
- Wine tasting

If you're more of a beach bum, you might consider classes in scuba diving, wind surfing or sailing. But how do you find classes in your hobby or interests?

A good travel agent knows where to find packages offering study-tour combinations. Tell your agent what subjects and countries you're interested in, or check the extension course catalogue at a local university. One year, for example, the art department at the University of California at Los Angeles (UCLA) offered three-week sessions at the Royal College of Art in London. Classes covered art history, drawing, painting, photography, sculpture and interior design. Field trips included visits to museums and historic buildings. Study courses can vary each year and have included such titles as Tropical Ecology in the Amazon, and the Land of the Pharaohs in Egypt.

In addition to the travel experience, the course credits earned and the friendships developed with fellow students, there is a special feeling that comes from immersion in another culture—the feeling that you have *lived* in a place, not simply *visited* it.

Classes will add to the cost of your trip, but you would pay for the same class at home. And without the extra travel incentive, you may never take the class at all. Of course, participation in a class may require that you stay in one place for the duration of the course and limit your travel and your side trips.

If you prefer to keep moving while you study, you can participate in a seminar at sea. Twice my husband and I participated in an investment seminar cruise, he as a speaker and I as travel coordinator. The seminar attracted both singles and couples who spent two or three hours a day learning about stocks and bonds, real estate investments, wills and trusts. The rest of the time we enjoyed the various ports of call in the Caribbean or Alaska as well as the ship's facilities.

Sometimes, a cruise line will sponsor and advertise a seminar, and sometimes a local or national organization such as the American Medical Association may offer on-board courses and publicize them through its mailing lists.

Cultivating Friendships Abroad

When I first met Rudy and Sylvia Haber at a hotel in Istanbul, they were midway into an around-the-world trip. We discovered that they lived a few blocks from my parents in southern California, and I invited them to visit me when they reached Rome, where I was living and working at the time. They did, and we became fast friends. The Habers made many friends that trip. Aside from having a familiarity with Spanish, the Habers spoke only English, but they were outgoing, gregarious and interested in people. Whenever they returned to Europe or Asia, they had a myriad of people to visit or stay with, enriching the memories brought home.

Even if you're not particularly outgoing and gregarious, you can make contacts on your trip if you take some steps in advance. First, talk to your relatives and friends about your destinations and ask them if they know anyone there. If your boss starts to tell you about his Uncle Gerhard in Cologne, say, "I'll be in Cologne on Tuesday, shall I call him for you?" In other words, show that you are open to meeting others.

One way to make friends abroad is by staying with a family in their home. The American Field Service arranges home stays for exchange students. Home Stay or Farm Stay tours are also offered for all ages by some countries, including Ireland, New Zealand, Australia and Israel.

Perhaps you work for a company with a branch in another city or country. Call or write to a colleague in that office and introduce yourself. Tell the colleague when you will be in town and ask if you can visit the branch office. Whatever your business or career at home, you can probably find a counterpart abroad and set up appointments to initiate contacts with other people.

Prior to a trip through Scandinavia, an American language teacher from Boston wrote to the language departments of a few schools in Sweden asking if she could observe their teaching methods. At one of her appointments she met a teacher who had visited relatives living in Boston. When the American mentioned that she was headed for Finland, the Swedish teacher invited her home for dinner and introduced her sister and brother-in-law who were also headed to Finland on vacation. The three made the overnight ferry journey together and still keep in touch. While there is no guarantee that such contacts will develop into friendships, they can at least be a starting point for meeting locals.

Follow up these meetings with thank you letters and offer to reciprocate. Also, if you are the recipient of Uncle Gerhard's hospitality or anyone else's, you should offer to pay for your share of food and automobile expenses, particularly if you stay in someone's home. When you accept the hospitality of others, you imply your willingness to do the same for them. Don't be surprised, then, if Uncle Gerhard sends relatives or friends your way to be entertained.

Maintaining friendships over long distances requires that you keep in touch by telephone, letters, e-mail or personal emissary. In other words, cultivating friendships takes a certain amount of work. But if you like people, it's work you will enjoy.

TAKING CARE OF YOURSELF

Table for One

My first night in Milan, Italy, I dined alone at a lovely restaurant that had been recommended. As it was somewhat late and not many patrons were left in the room, the waiters hovered around, asking if I wanted this or that. We were all, it seemed, delighted to have someone to chat with. For some, however, the worst part of traveling alone is dining alone. Feeling self-conscious, some travelers bury their heads in a magazine or book as if not looking at anyone will make them inconspicuous. Although there's no real reason to feel awkward eating alone, there are a few alternatives if you do.

You can pass up the fine dining restaurants and opt for the counter in a coffee shop, grab some take-out at a fast-food outlet or call for room service or pizza delivery. Another alternative is to choose a restaurant with window tables, requesting one when you make your reservation. This way, you can sit facing the view and not feel like people are looking at you.

Other single travelers avoid dining out, not because they feel awkward, but because some restaurants routinely shuffle them to the worst table in the house—the tiny one with the uneven legs in the back of the restaurant facing the stack of dirty dishes. While it may appear that the maitre d' has personally singled them out for this ignominious honor, it may simply be a matter of practicality. Two people seated at the tiny table would be more uncomfortable than one, and one person unhappy with the view is better than two or more unhappy people. Or it may be that since one person eats less and is unlikely to order a bottle of wine, that person is relegated to a table commensurate with the bill.

A businessman who enjoys fine dining when traveling has found a successful strategy for getting a good table. Sometime during the day he passes by the restaurant he has targeted for dinner, often located in his hotel, and checks the menu, the layout of the room and the name of the maitre d'. When calling for a reservation he requests a table "by the potted plants" or "by the window on the right side." When he approaches the maitre d', he uses his name, "Jerry, have you got my table for me?" The maitre d' assumes the businessman is a regular patron and gives him a decent table.

"I Vant to Be Alone"

For the lone traveler who wants to be alone, there are certain rules of the road. A young woman by herself in an English pub is just that and nothing more. But a single woman who sits at a bar in the United States implies to some that she's looking for company. If she's not, it's best to sit at a table. Likewise, a man at a nightclub or bar in some parts of Asia is apt to find one of the "house ladies" inviting him to buy her a drink. So before you venture out into unknown territory, familiarize yourself with the local customs by reading travel books about your destination.

Safety

What can you do to feel safer when traveling alone? One client of mine, a woman in her thirties who travels frequently on business, insists on hotels with rooms that open to an inside corridor and not to an outside parking area or balcony. You can buy portable security devices that attach to any hotel door and electronic sensors that trigger an alarm when they detect motion.

If you don't want to find yourself walking or waiting for transportation on lonely streets at night, anticipate how you will get from one place to another. Once when I was in New York on business, I took a cab to the theater alone. I knew that after the performance it would be difficult to find a taxi because of the crowds exiting the various theaters. So I left the theater just as the curtain was coming down and was the first person out the door.

Coming from southern California, however, I failed to anticipate the sudden summer storm that greeted me. It was pouring and there wasn't a cab in sight, only a long queue of limousines waiting for the fortunate few. When I sighted a taxi down the block, I lost it to some fierce competition. As the crowd thinned, I grew nervous that I would have to walk back to the hotel through dark, empty streets. The only alternative was to become more aggressive.

The next time a hint of yellow paint flashed at the corner, I sprinted to the cab and arrived at the door simultaneously with three other people. We agreed to share it.

While you can't anticipate every obstacle that can arise, be sure to think ahead, not only about getting to your destination but also about getting back. The next time you go to the theater alone, you can hire a limousine if you're feeling flush or arrange with the cab company in advance to pick you up across the street from the theater, where it will be easier to find you in the crowd.

Remember to leave a copy of your itinerary with a family member or friend, and if on an extended trip, call home or the office if feasible each time you change cities. This way, if you disappear, someone will know where to start looking. If you are in a foreign city and decide to go on your own into a rural or undeveloped area, alert the closest American consulate of your plans and notify your contact when you return. There are, of course, some places you should never go unescorted unless you are an expert on the area. You would not search out gorillas in Africa, for example, or hike into the jungles of the Amazon without a qualified guide. Should you have any doubt about the safety of traveling alone to any destination, ask your travel agent or someone else who knows the area well.

If You Get Sick

John, a client in his mid-60s, has chronic heart problems. Nonetheless, he travels around the world on his own every summer, stopping in exotic places such as Bhutan, Mongolia and Kenya, to name a few. Before we finalize his itinerary, John notes the altitude at his planned destinations and checks with his doctor.

As always, the best medicine is prevention. If you have medical problems that could result in illness while abroad, it's wise to consult with your doctor before traveling alone.

Of course, even healthy persons can get sick or have an accident while traveling. While most deluxe hotels will have a doctor on staff, you may not be able to communicate easily or read the label on the prescribed medicine—medicine that might not meet U.S. standards. If you prefer an English-speaking doctor, the American consulate in each country can usually provide a list of recommended physicians. A supply of headache, stomach and antibiotic medications won't take up much room in your suitcase. Nor will an extra pair of glasses or contact lenses.

Check Your Smile

Suppose you're shopping for a new stereo and you see two salesmen in the shop. One wears a scowl and waits for you to approach him. The other smiles and says, "Good morning. May I help you?" Which salesman will get your business?

If your preference is to meet people when you travel, remember that it's natural for us to gravitate to people who appear warm and friendly. Even if you're naturally shy, other people may be shy too. Hanging out your smile is like hanging out a sign that says "You can talk to me. I won't bite." People tend to be open to you if you appear open to them. So check your smile now and then.

And if, on the other hand, you don't wish to meet people or invite intrusions into your time and space, you can usually signal this preference in various ways. On a plane or a train, for example, it may be as easy as involving yourself in a book, rather than looking up and around. Often we can project a "business only" attitude just by the way we stand, walk or ask questions. Learning to convey your disposition successfully is part of the art of traveling by yourself.

TEN

How to Survive Traveling with Your Pet

Advantages

One advantage of taking your pet along when you travel is that you won't have to worry about its care while you're away. Is Fifi receiving the proper food and exercise from your next-door neighbor? Will Fido be lonely in the kennel without your tender loving care? These are some of the questions that might plague you if you leave your pet behind—and factors you can control if your pet is with you.

Sometimes it's not only your pet's well-being you worry about. A client who left his dog with his parents when he went to Canada was awakened at 6 A.M. by a telephone call from his father. In 24 hours his Dalmatian had dug up his father's rare-orchid garden, chewed his mother's $60 designer sunglasses and terrorized the postman. The son cut his vacation short and returned home before the damages, which already exceeded $500, could make this trip his most expensive yet. Another advantage of taking your pet with you is peace of mind, knowing that when you return, you won't wind up "in the dog house."

Travel with your pet can also provide opportunities to meet people. Strangers will have a tendency to stop you on the street and begin a conversation. When fellow pet lovers run into each other, they already have a common bond that transcends language and nationality.

"What a great looking dog."

"Rover's a wolf."

"I have a dog that looks just like yours."

"Rover's a wolf."

"That's a great name for a dog."

"Rover's a wolf."

Your pet can be a conversation piece that immediately links you with strangers. There's something trustworthy about a person with a pet, unless the pet happens to be a pit bull or boa constrictor.

Some people travel with their pets, lovable or not, for the feeling of security in a strange place. Of course, if your pet is a parakeet, you can't count on much security, but it may keep you company, particularly if you're traveling alone.

Disadvantages

The main disadvantage of traveling with your pet is the limitation placed on where you stay, where you eat, where you go and how you get there. You may have to content yourself with sleeping in a tent or a camper, for example, if you can't find a hotel or motel at your destination that accepts pets. If you do find one, it may not offer the degree of comfort you prefer when traveling by yourself.

Since the majority of hotels and motels don't accept pets, you'll have to spend time researching and planning the trip and, in some cases, gathering the necessary papers and shots for your pet. And although it may not cost you as much as taking a child, bringing your pet along will require time and attention while traveling, time you might otherwise have all to yourself.

CONSIDERATIONS

Where Can We Go?

Sherry, a client who lives in California, takes the same vacation every year. Every summer she packs up herself and her two cats and goes back to Ohio where the family welcomes her and "tolerates" the two cats. "I'd love to go somewhere else for a change, but I wouldn't leave my cats behind. Where else can I go?"

The answer to the question "Where can I go with my pet?" depends on three other questions: Is quarantine required? Where can we stay? and How will we get there?

Is Quarantine Required?

If you stay within the confines of the mainland United States or Alaska, you don't have to worry about quarantine requirements for your pet. Hawaii, however, has a 120-day quarantine period for any pets from the mainland. That would tend to eliminate Hawaii as a destination, unless, of course, you're taking a year-long vacation. Even then, you may find the cost of quarantine prohibitive. When you travel to a place that requires quarantine, it is up to you to reserve the kennel space and pay the fees for the duration of the quarantine period. These fees can run about $815 for a cat and $875 for a dog.

Quarantine requirements vary from country to country and range anywhere from about 10 days to 6 months. You can check this requirement by writing or calling the consulate of the country you are planning to visit. (A travel agent can direct you to the consulate closest to you.) Once you know that quarantine restrictions won't eliminate your destination, you're ready to tackle question number two.

Where Can We Stay?

Finding hotels or motels that welcome pets will take a little research. Guide books published by the American Automobile Association (AAA) detail which establishments accept pets. These Tour-Books cover all of the United States and are issued free to AAA members. Check your local bookstore for other guide books that detail accommodations welcoming pets at your destination.

You can also check with your travel agent. In addition to hotel books, most travel agency computer systems can access hotel listings around the world, and although these lists may not be complete, pet acceptance is noted where applicable. Keep in mind that because computer services charge hotels for the listing, many smaller, less expensive places, such as bed and breakfast lodgings, cannot afford to be listed. And sometimes it's these more casual hostelries run by moms and pops that accept pets.

Don't assume that if one hotel in a chain accepts pets, it's a standard practice for the hotel chain. In most cases, a blanket policy does not exist. For example, the Hilton Palmer House in Chicago currently accepts small pets, but the Chicago Hilton and Towers doesn't.

Hotel policies also differ from country to country. In the United States, for example, many luxury hotels do not accept pets while in Paris, pets are accepted at a number of deluxe hotels including the Crillon and the Ritz.

If you can't find a place to stay that accepts pets, you can, of course, still travel to the destination. You'll just need to bring your own housing. You can rent a recreational vehicle or pitch your tent in the nearest campground.

If you do find accommodations where pets are accepted, don't assume that your pet peacock will be welcome to prance around the property. Many lodgings that accept pets really mean small, well-behaved dogs or cats. If your pet is unusually large like a Great Dane, unusually noisy like a screeching parrot, or just unusual, call the property first and make sure your pet will be acceptable.

If you're unfamiliar with the hotel or motel, the following are questions to ask that will help you determine if it's appropriate to bring your pet:

1. Can my pet stay in my room or must it stay outside? Tell the hotel what kind of pet you have. The hotel reservationist may be imagining a cocker spaniel and not your four-foot-high Doberman pinscher.

2. Does the hotel have kennels on the property? Is there space outdoors for pets? Is it fenced? Will other pets be fenced in as well? This could be important if your dog likes to make mince-meat out of other people's cats.

3. Are the rooms all located in one building or in separate cottages? If your dog barks at every stranger who walks up and down the hallway, you can both quickly become *personae non gratae*. On the other hand, if your room is in a detached cottage, your dog is less likely to disturb others and vice versa.

4. Is there a charge for the pet? Some lodgings allow pets free of charge while others require a fee.

Camping is an alternative for those who like the outdoors. Most U.S. campgrounds and state parks welcome pets. A guide book to camp areas will usually indicate which campgrounds accept pets. Some charge a small fee. If you plan to camp in a national or state park, you can check with the state's Office of Parks and Recreation.

Pet policies differ from park to park. You'll need to keep your dog on a leash, and some campgrounds require that your dogs remain inside your tent or camper at night.

Never take your pet for a hike into woods where bears or other dangerous animals might be present. If your dog runs ahead of you into a bear and a chase ensues, your dog may come running right back to you bringing the bear on its heels.

A few major tourist areas like Grand Canyon National Park and Disneyland provide kennel facilities for a fee so sightseers can park their pet for a few hours while they tour the attraction.

Dining with Your Pet

When I was a kid, my grandmother had a cocker spaniel named Nicky. Theoretically, Nicky was not to eat at the family table. But Nicky was always there, stretching tall on his hind legs by our chairs, paws out, begging with sad eyes. No one was supposed to feed Nicky pasta with meatballs, but someone always did. So Nicky the Nuisance was always at the table or, rather, just slightly below it.

Although you may be used to sharing your dinner with your pet in your home, feeding it from the table is not acceptable etiquette when dining elsewhere. If you are taking advantage of the hospitality of relatives, don't assume your pet is welcome at their table.

Just because Aunt Betsy and Cousin Will are related to you doesn't mean they feel akin to your pet. Some people lose their appetites entirely when animals are present around food. Pet etiquette requires that you put the dog or cat out of the room when you're eating, even if your hosts don't request it. While the host may be a pet lover, others at the table may not appreciate your pet under their feet at meal time.

Most people won't appreciate your pet wandering anywhere in the house or patio where food is left out in the open. I once attended a cocktail party where hors d'oeuvres had been set out in a living room thick with guests in three-piece suits and dressy dresses. When the host opened the door to his garage to get something, his excited beagle ran into the house. Before the host could collar it, the dog romped around the guests, setting loose a cascade of tiny silver balls from one beaded dress and leaving paw prints on another. Shooed away, it made a beeline for a large, expensive wheel of cheddar, took a few licks and headed for the canapés. Although the host didn't see the dog get its licks in, the guests did, and no one went near the hors d'oeuvres the rest of the evening.

If you are lucky enough to have relatives or friends accept you and your pet as house guests, don't abuse the invitation by allowing your pet the run of the house. It's up to you to look after it at all times. In fact, it's a good idea to ask up front, "Where can I keep Lucifer?" This way, if your sister-in-law says, "There's plenty of room in the yard," you'll have a good indication she doesn't expect to see Lucifer in the house, and there will be no misunderstandings.

Although it's not unusual to see patrons dining with their dogs or cats in many restaurants in France, pets are rarely welcome in restaurants in the United States. If you're traveling by car and staying at lodgings, you'll need to feed your own pet. Place the food and water dishes in the bathroom to avoid any stains on the rug and remember to clean up when he forgets his table manners.

Getting There by Plane

If you want to travel with your pet by plane within the continental United States, check the airline's pet policies first. These policies vary per carrier and equipment. Southwest Airlines does not, for example, accept pets (except those trained for the blind or deaf). Although United Airlines accepts pets, United's commuter link, United Express, may place stricter limits on the size or the number of kennels permitted on smaller aircraft. Since policies can change, always check in advance.

There are two ways your pet can accompany you on airlines that accept pets:

1. Pet in cabin

2. Pet in cargo

PET IN CABIN

If your pet is a small domestic cat, dog or bird, you can request approval for pet in cabin. How small? Small enough to fit in a kennel under the seat in front of you. While this space may vary depending on the type of equipment, usually the kennel can be no larger than 23"L x 13"W x 9"H and your pet must be able to stand up and turn around inside.

Most airlines will only allow one or two pets per cabin, so make your reservations as early as possible. While some airlines require that your pet remain in the kennel only during boarding, takeoff and landing, others require that the animal be confined throughout the flight.

"Why can't I just hide my kitten in my pocket or purse?" one traveler wanted to know. In this age of security checks, you probably don't want your pet going through the x-ray machine, and woe be to you if your Lhasa apso bites the hand that's searching your purse or carry-on piece.

Of course, some passengers have been known to sneak their pets out of the kennel into their laps in violation of the rules. One client was bringing home a surprise puppy for his daughter. Once on board, he surreptitiously removed the puppy from the kennel under the seat and placed it inside a *Wall Street Journal* he had rolled into a funnel with a rubber band at one end. He placed it on the empty seat next to him between a pillow and the armrest. Every time the puppy gave a little yap, the passenger on the other side would look around the cabin seeking the source of this strange sound.

"Did you hear that?" he asked.

"Hear what?" The client coughed and cleared his throat to cover up the barking.

As the client describes it, "The other passenger thought he was losing his mind. Several times, he got up and walked around the cabin, his eyes darting up and down. By the time we landed, he was in a sweat. I picked up my newspaper by the bottom of the funnel and carried it out with the empty kennel. The confused passenger pointed to the kennel victoriously and said, 'Ah ha! You're the one with the dog. I knew I heard barking.'

"Oh this?" I replied, opening the case. "It's empty. See? It's my daughter's. I'm bringing it out from our apartment on the East Coast.

"The other man turned pale and the smile left his face until I showed him the puppy in the paper. He shook his head. 'I really thought I was going crazy there for a while,' he said and disappeared into the crowd, laughing."

If a flight attendant had seen the puppy, she might not have been amused. If you don't comply with the regulations, the crew can ask you to leave the plane. And if they have to make a special landing so you can leave, you won't be laughing either.

PET IN CARGO

The other way to take your pet along with you on a flight is pet in cargo. To arrange for your pet to be checked into the baggage compartment, you'll need to do the following:

1. When you make your own airline reservations, request approval on each segment of the trip for your pet in cargo. This way, you'll be sure in advance that the airline in question accepts pets and knows how many to expect.

2. Ask the reservationist what the charges are for the pet. Rates currently are around $35-50 each way for flights within the United States. This means that if you are flying to Grand Rapids round trip with a connection through Chicago, the cost to fly your pet in cargo at $50 each way will be $100 (plus the cost of the kennel, if you don't have your own). However, if you change carriers when making the connections in Chicago, you have to pay for each segment separately, or a total of $200. This amount can be paid at the check-in counter by cash or credit card. Personal checks are usually accepted with a photo identification and major credit card. If a parent or someone beside yourself will be paying for the pet's transportation, you can arrange that in advance with a travel agent. The payee pays the travel agent who then issues a payment document called an MCO (Miscellaneous Charges Order), which the airline will accept as payment for the pet upon check-in. Since travel agents receive no commission on this transaction from the airline, don't be surprised if they ask you to pay a service charge.

3. If you don't have your own kennel, tell the reservationist what size you will need and check the cost. Most airlines sell a variety of sizes ranging from about 17"L x 12"W x 7"H to a maximum of about 40"L x 27"W x 30"H for miniature horses. Depending on their size, kennels run from about $20 to $75. Your pet must be able to stand and turn around in the kennel, and his weight combined with the kennel's should not exceed the airline's maximum, which is about 182 pounds. If you are using a kennel purchased elsewhere, be sure it is leakproof, fastens securely, provides good ventilation, is sturdy and has an absorbent bottom. Those made of plastic or fiberglass are usually considered better than metal ones, because metal conducts heat and cold faster. Unless you're an expert

craftsperson, this is not the time to economize by building your own. For your pet's safety, you want to be sure the kennel meets United States Department of Agriculture standards.

4. Ask if any documents are required. Even within the continental United States, some airlines may require that you have with you a certificate, signed by a veterinarian and dated within 10 days of the flight (date requirement varies), specifying that your animal (a) is free from disease and (b) has a current rabies shot. (The definition of current varies from state to state and depends on the type of vaccine used.)

Although airline officials may not ask to see the document, they will usually ask if you have it.

TO TRANQUILIZE OR NOT TO TRANQUILIZE

The decision to tranquilize your pet or not is one your veterinarian should help you make. Tranquilizing is generally *not* recommended because it lowers an animal's body temperature. While temperatures in pressurized cargo holds usually range between 50 and 70 degrees Fahrenheit, they can, in extreme circumstances, drop as low as 35 degrees.

On the other hand, if your pet tends to be very fearful or excitable, sedation may be advisable. The medication is in pill form and given to the pet approximately one hour prior to the flight. Most tranquilizers will have a maximum effect of six to eight hours.

Be sure to get the proper dosage and instructions from your vet. If your dog tends to bark and will be carried into the cabin, you may want to give it a sedative. The flight attendants could refuse to board a barking or howling dog. If you and your vet decide to tranquilize your pet for a flight, keep in mind that your dog may act differently than usual.

When a friend let her tranquilized Doberman out of his kennel after a three-hour flight, the dog was still wobbly from the drug and could hardly stand up. He looked and acted drunk for several hours. Since she couldn't coax him back into the kennel, she had to carry him to the car.

DO'S AND DON'TS

Below is a list of do's and don'ts to help you avoid problems when traveling by plane with your pet.

1. Don't release your pet from the kennel inside the airport terminal no matter how anxious you both are to greet each other.

A friend made the mistake of letting his dog out of the kennel while still inside the baggage claim area. The dog was so excited to see him, it immediately left a brown deposit on the floor. The friend tried to make a quick exit with his pet but was stopped by an official who spotted the unattractive heap.

"Did your dog make that mess?"

"My dog!" the owner responded, sounding incensed.

"This is a highly-bred, well-trained Labrador." Then, spotting another dog, he pointed to it. "I think it was that little poodle over there."

When the official marched over to the poodle's keeper, the Labrador and his owner disappeared quickly out the door.

No matter how well-trained your pet may be, its reactions to the abnormal circumstance of flying could take you by surprise. A normally docile pet, when nervous or agitated, may become aggressive and bite. One dog that was let out of its kennel while still in the terminal was frightened by luggage thumping down the rotating baggage carousel. The dog bolted down the hall and charged through the security checkpoint before the owner could collar it. They were delayed by security officials who were most interested in an explanation.

2. Don't feed your pet anything unusual before a flight.

   Dr. Julie Ryan, a southern California veterinarian, recommends that food be withheld for approximately eight hours prior to departure. Water should not be withheld, however, and you should walk your pet before placing it in the kennel. If you've never flown with your pet, you probably don't know if your pet is prone to air sickness, but if you know in advance that you could be flying in turbulent weather, ask your vet about sedation.

3. Do try to take nonstop flights when possible. This will lessen the time your pet has to spend in the kennel whether in flight or on the ground waiting to be loaded. If you can't avoid a change of planes, at least avoid switching carriers. If you transfer between two planes of the same carrier, your pet in cargo will be transferred for you. But if another carrier is involved, you will have to collect your pet from the first flight and check it in again for the connecting flight. If your connection is a close one, by the time you wait for your pet to be unloaded, you could miss the second flight. Or worse, you could make the connection, but your pet won't be loaded in time.

4. Don't take your pet on a flight if it's pregnant, frail, extremely nervous, less than six weeks old or weaned from its mother for less than a week.

5. Don't travel with your pet in extreme weather. While temperatures are regulated in the air, your pet could spend hours on the ground. Extreme heat could result in heat stroke. Severe storms could result in long delays. You don't want your pet cooped up in a kennel any longer than necessary. If your 5-hour flight is delayed an hour for bad weather, stands on the runway another hour waiting to be de-iced, and lands mid-

way in the journey to wait for a snow clearing at your destination airport, the 5 hours can easily become 10.

Sometimes passengers are housed overnight in airport hotels until weather permits the flight to proceed. What becomes of your pet in these cases? Airline policies vary, but the Animal Welfare Act requires that interstate carriers of animals meet certain standards of care. Temperatures in terminals where pets are held, for example, must be maintained between 45 and 75 degrees Fahrenheit. The law also requires carriers to feed dogs and cats every 24 hours and puppies and kittens every twelve hours.

At some airports, baggage handlers will take pets that haven't been picked up to a carrier's freight department for care. Or they turn them over to the operations department where loading decisions are made. In some cases, airlines will board the pets overnight at a kennel. An airline reservationist recalled the time one baggage-service manager took home a passel of kittens during a severe snowstorm because it was so cold in the terminal.

If you and your pet are separated on the ground for a long time, you can ask about retrieving your kennel. If this is not possible, you will have to hope that there's a caring person looking out for your pet. That's why it's a good idea to tag the kennel, not only with identification but also with information that includes your pet's name, type, and weight, along with the date and time of last feeding. You'll do baggage handlers a favor by also indicating whether your pet is likely to bite the hand that feeds it.

LOST PET

While lost or delayed luggage is a common occurrence, there's little chance of your pet ending up in El Paso when you're headed for Pittsburgh because unlike baggage, which is often loaded in pods, kennels are loaded by hand. That means that a human being has to read the tag to send your pet on the specified route.

Mistakes can and do occur occasionally, however. One man, an attorney whose pet didn't show up in baggage claim, threatened to sue the airline for his pet's pain and suffering if it wasn't found immediately. As it turned out, the dog had never been loaded on the flight and was flown up on the next one.

There are other hazards, to be sure. If the airline ventilation system fails for some reason, your pet could be asphyxiated or have a bad reaction to fumes from insecticides used in the cargo hold. If your pet has trouble breathing to begin with, it's probably wiser to leave it at home. On the other hand, thousands of healthy pets have become frequent travelers with no ill effects.

INTERNATIONAL FLIGHTS

If you want to fly out of the country with your pet, the first step is to check with the consulate or embassy of your destination country for

1. quarantine restrictions and costs

2. required papers, including rabies certificates, visas or licenses

If your pet will be quarantined for a time, you'll have to arrange to have it met at customs and transferred to the quarantine kennel, which may require advance payment of fees in the local currency. Depending on the country, your pet may need a license or the prior approval of the country's consulate, the equivalent of a visa, for entry. Other countries like Holland merely require a certificate of good health and a rabies certificate written in English or Dutch.

In addition to meeting the foreign country's quarantine and certification requirements, you'll need to check that an airline serving that destination will transport your pet and that you meet any specific requirements of that carrier. Don't assume that an airline that accepts pets in the cabin or in baggage domestically will also accept them internationally. Although American, Continental and United Airlines will take small pets in the cabin domestically, they cannot do so on flights to the United Kingdom because England's law prohibits the transport of pets in cabins. (Animals can be flown as excess baggage, however.)

Be sure to check costs. On international flights, pets are usually charged as excess baggage. The cost to take your pet along to Vienna, for example, runs around $121 for a smaller animal and around $240 if the kennel is bigger than 62 inches total length and girth.

When you re-enter the United States, you have to show a current rabies certificate, and your pet has to "look healthy" to the public health personnel or customs official on duty. Without proper documentation, your pet may be warehoused until quarantine can be arranged. In some cities like Los Angeles, you would have to contact a customs broker to arrange for a bond before the animal can even be transported to quarantine.

In other words, three sets of standards must be met: (1) the destination country's, (2) the airline carrier's and (3) the United States Department of Agriculture's (USDA).

Getting There by Car

The advantage of traveling with your pet by car is that you can stop when you wish to walk your dog or feed your rabbit. If your goal, however, is to make as few stops as possible along the way, be sure to exercise your pet before the trip, and unless it's very hot, give your pet its last drink a couple of hours before you start. Here are a few items to bring along.

1. Food and water dishes.

2. A supply of usual pet food. The supply size will depend on accessibility to stores along your route and how much time you prefer to spend shopping versus traveling. This is not the time to try a new brand and discover your pet is allergic to it.

3. A gallon container of emergency water (ice water if the weather is hot) that can be refilled along the way. Of course, you should bring along a gallon for yourself, too, in case your car breaks down in an isolated area.

4. Kennel, cage or litter box. Even if your pet will be free in the backseat, you may need a kennel at your destination, particularly if you plan to leave your pet alone at times in a motel or hotel room. More than one unsuspecting maid, perceived as an intruder, has been forced to flee an attacking dog.

5. A leash for walking your pet at stops along the way. Your pet's first inclination after being in a confined space may be to run off some pent-up energy. Without a leash, your pet can race into unfamiliar territory before you can stop it.

6. Your pet's favorite toy or bone. In a place where everything else is different, a familiar toy can help your pet feel more secure.

7. Health certificate and proof of rabies shots or feline leukemia vaccine for cats. Some kennels, campgrounds and parks may require them for entry.

8. Any usual medications prescribed by your vet according to your pet's weight. Don't give it human medications just because they work for you.

9. Cleaning supplies including soap, water, paper towels, pooper-scooper, and club soda to help take pet prints off car seats.

If your pet is young or new to you, be sure it has been around the block a few times in your car before you plan a long trip. Otherwise, neither of you will know what to expect. Will your pet lie quietly curled up on the seat or jump around the car and interfere with your driving? Will it get carsick?

A friend took her Doberman, Buckles, on a trip up the

California coast with her children. The highway was renowned for curves as well as spectacular views.

"I should have paid attention to the warning signs," Joan says. "Buckles was swinging his head from side to side and his eyes were rolling around. He would lean the wrong way into the curves, and even his black coat looked a little green. I should have stopped right then and taken him for a walk, before he got carsick all over me, the kids and the station wagon. After that, whenever we took Buckles on a long trip, I called the vet for medication and watched him for those telltale signs."

To avoid car sickness, feed your pet at the end of the trip or in the evenings when you stop for the day. Experience with your pet in the car during short trips will help reduce unpleasant surprises for both of you when you vacation together.

SAFETY ON THE ROAD

If your pet will remain in a kennel or cage while traveling, be sure it's set securely on the floor or wedged in on the backseat so it can't fall off. Unless your pet will be held in another passenger's lap or ride in a kennel, be sure it stays in the backseat.

For fresh air, keep the windows open a few inches but not enough that your pet can stick its body out. By the way, you might want to keep two different kennels: one that meets air travel regulations and a wire mesh kennel that will permit maximum air circulation during car travel.

Never leave your pet alone in the car on a hot day. Even with the windows open a few inches, the temperature inside the car can soar higher than the outside temperature. If you don't have air conditioning, plan to stop more frequently in hot weather to give your pet water and a chance to cool down.

Getting There by Ship

In one of those old movies from the '30s or '40s, two wealthy matrons walked their dogs on the promenade deck of a transatlantic ocean liner. An episode from a television series featured a dog show on board the ship. While images like these may give the impression that pets are welcome guests aboard ship, a survey of cruise lines reveals that pets are rarely accepted. The television episode referred to, for example, was filmed in a sound studio, not on board a Princess cruise ship as depicted in the episode. With the exception of dogs and monkeys that serve the handicapped, Princess Cruises does not accept pets.

Few ships sailing from U.S. ports will accept pets. Cunard Line's Queen Elizabeth II (QE 2) is an exception. The QE 2 accepts cats and dogs that are no larger than a German shepherd on transatlantic crossings. The pets remain in the ship's kennel and are walked and fed by the kennel master or kennel maid. Passengers can visit their pets and play with them but can't take them out of the kennel area.

Pet fares are around $500 for dogs and cats. However, passengers crossing the Atlantic with pets will have to disembark in France or another continental port and skip England if they want to avoid the English six-month quarantine rule.

Although most freighters that carry passengers do not accept pets because of possible quarantine delays, a number of ship lines linking European ports do accept pets. Silja Line, for example, accepts pets between Stockholm and Helsinki.

In sum, unless one of a few ships that accepts pets happens to be going your way, you may have to buy or build your own ark to cruise with your pet.

Getting There by Train or Bus

Except for service/guide dogs for the deaf and blind, bus lines and trains in the United States are not equipped to transport pets. According to Amtrak, baggage cars are not heated or ventilated. Federal law prohibits animals in the passenger compartments.

Your pet can travel by train in Canada, but only in baggage. Europe, however, is far more accommodating when it comes to pets. In France, Italy and Germany, for example, your dog or cat can stay with you in the cabin for a fee that varies. Some countries require that dogs be muzzled or carried in a kennel or, at a minimum, stay on a leash.

What happens if the pet makes a mess? Even if your dog is well trained, when you take it on a foreign train, be sure you carry a pooper-scooper, lest your pet perpetuate the image of the "Ugly American" with the "Ugly American Dog."

WHEN YOUR PET IS A HORSE

Unless you charter the aircraft, you and your horse cannot travel together by scheduled airline. Except for miniatures, horses are not accepted in baggage. They can, however, be shipped separately as cargo, usually in lots of three or more. Costs for their quarantine can be substantial. A client who purchased an Icelandic Pony while on vacation in Reykjavik felt fortunate that the United States required only five days quarantine for his new pet. Still, at $100 a day, these fees added to the cost of hauling the pony west equaled the purchase price.

When your pet is a horse, one way to travel together is to invest in a horse trailer that you can hitch to your car or truck.

When professional horse people—rodeo riders, horse breeders, racehorse owners, trainers, stable owners, cowboys—hit the road, they are usually destined for a corral or stables where their horses will be boarded. If, however, you just want to take your horse along so you can ride during your vacation, you'll have to do some research to find stables along your route willing to board your horse overnight.

Most ranch guide books list the locations where horseback riding is offered. You can start by checking with these stables. If they won't board your horse, they probably know who, if anyone, in the area will. Make these arrangements in advance and don't forget to bring a health certificates, copies of breeding papers, water and feed for the road, saddle, blankets, buckets and shovel.

One way to lessen the cost of traveling with your horse is to camp out at designated horse camps. One such camp, Manzanita, at Montana de Oro State Park near Morro Bay, California, provides stalls and water for horses by the campsite, a fire pit and table for $16 a night (reservations required). Some horse camps are designed for groups of 20 or more horse riders, so horse lovers can travel together and ride together. The difference when camping out rather than boarding the horse is that you will have to haul enough feed for your entire stay, and that can be a bulky proposition. Your state Department of Parks and Recreation can usually provide a list of camping sites that permit horses for a small fee.

WHEN YOUR PET IS A CELLO

I met a musician at a party who played with the Los Angeles Philharmonic and sometimes with the studios when they recorded scores for films and television. He asked me that evening to make his plane reservation to New York for one such engagement and added, "Make a reservation for my cello too."

"You don't need a reservation for baggage," I told him.

"Baggage!" Purple veins protruded over his bulging eyes as he waved his arms like a referee calling an incomplete pass. "No. No.

Never! We're not just talking cello here. We're talking *Guarneri*." He plucked each syllable like staccato notes. "It's priceless. Trust it to the untrained, uncaring hands of baggage handlers? Never! Reserve a seat, please, for my cello right next to me."

And so I did. Since he was traveling first class, the cost for the cello was 100 percent of the first class fare. Had he traveled in coach, he would have paid 100 percent of the regular unrestricted coach fare.

Does this mean you can buy a ticket for Aunt Betsy's antique lamp or your son's computer? Requirements differ from airline to airline, but except for smaller aircraft, most airlines will allow you to buy a seat for an item you don't want in baggage, provided it fits in the seat and presents no hazard.

You may wonder, If I can buy a seat for a cello, why not for my full-grown sheep dog? Several years ago, a client found himself seated in first class next to Lassie. Which brings us to the final point. Airlines do sometimes make exceptions even if your pet isn't a star.

Delta Airlines broke its own rules when it transported a miniature schnauzer puppy sans owner or other paying passenger from Portland to Los Angeles. The Schnauzer was a replacement for the owner's service dog that had died. A doctor had prescribed the dog to help the owner overcome a chemically-based depressive fear anytime she left home or family.

Unless you have an equally compelling reason, don't expect the airlines to bend their rules for you. Learning to cope with a myriad of regulations is part of the art of traveling with your pet.

Bon Voyage

It's vacation time. Hooray! Your friends just described their amazing trip to Italy's Amalfi coast. Already you can picture yourself there, dancing under the stars on the isle of Capri, sipping *limongello* on a balcony overlooking the beach in Positano. It will be your second honeymoon. You're so excited, you call your spouse and agree to meet after work in the travel section at a local book store. When you get there, however, your spouse is leafing through books on golf and is excited about playing some of Europe's best links, which, unfortunately, are not in Capri or Positano.

But you're ready with a solution. You know that your spouse, an avid golfer, will suffer withdrawal away from a golf course more than three days. You suggest three days of golfing near Edinburgh, Scotland, before you head to southern Italy. Yes, it's a compromise. But the joy of traveling and the joy of discovery are treasures worth sharing. So you both make the effort to accommodate each other.

Traveling with companions, even the ones you love, can produce more tense moments than the adventures of Indiana Jones, particularly if you are different types of travelers. Fortunately, you can find ways to make your trip enjoyable, not only for yourself but for those you travel with.

To do that, you need to understand that each of the nine

different types of travelers—the travel enthusiast, adventurer, sportsman, relaxer, beach bum, comfort seeker, culturist, shopper or explorer—has different expectations. What makes a trip a success for one is not necessarily true for the other. Just as you consult guidebooks to steer you to the right hotel, restaurant or antique shop, you now have a survival guide to help you travel successfully with your spouse, lover, boss, friends, kids, someone else's kids, parents, in-laws and other relatives and your pet as well as yourself. This book offers you ideas on how to anticipate and resolve potential conflicts that arise when travelers with different expectations end up on the road together.

Sometimes you can't compromise your vacation plans. But finding ways to blend together different ideas and activities to satisfy your needs and someone else's needs can be the greatest boon of all. Then you'll have the power to create a memorable travel experience not only for yourself but for your companions.

So break in your walking shoes, pack up the kids, Grandma and Rover and get ready to travel with others without wishing they'd stayed home.

Packing Tips for Trips of 7-21 Days

Baggage Allowances

Most airlines in the United States permit passengers to check three luggage pieces free of charge: the first not to exceed 62 inches when the height, width and length are added together; the second not to exceed 55 inches; and the third not to exceed 45 inches. No single bag may exceed 70 pounds. Some sports equipment such as golf clubs, fishing tackle or ski equipment is generally permitted in addition to or in lieu of one bag.

One of these bags may also be carried in the cabin provided it can be stowed in the overhead bin or under the seat—usually about 9"H x 13"W x 22"L. You may also carry free of charge a coat, purse, umbrella, camera, binoculars, reading material, infant food, luggage carrier, cane, crutches or collapsible walker.

Allowances on flights between the United States and a foreign city are similar, but checked bags are limited to two not to exceed 62 inches total. However, between two foreign cities, allowances are based primarily on weight. For example, between Paris and Nice, the limit is 50 pounds. Within Kenya, baggage on some flights to game parks is limited to 22 pounds.

In other words, travelers flying from a U.S. gateway to a foreign country and then to another destination within that country must satisfy both weight and inch requirements or be subject to excess baggage charges.

Keep a Packing List

The first time you travel for more than a few days, you may need to purchase new items that will help you maximize your wardrobe within a minimum of cubic inches. However, once you have planned trips to warm, cool and cold climates, subsequent planning will be minimal. All you have to do is keep your packing lists and update the items that need replacement each time you travel.

Limit Travel Wardrobe to One or Two Basic Colors

If you coordinate your travel clothes to one or two basic colors, you'll limit the number of accessories, such as shoes, ties or purses, you need to take. Since every color dress or suit will go with either navy blue, black, brown or beige shoes, you can limit the shoes you carry in your suitcase to the following:

1. Tennis shoes (for active vacationers)
2. Slippers (beach sandals can double as slippers)
3. Pair of shoes in the first basic color you choose.

You can wear the second color in transit. Women who feel comfortable shopping or sightseeing in tennis shoes won't need another pair of casual walking shoes. If they prefer, however, they can take a pair of low-heeled shoes for daytime and a dressier pair for evening and still pack no more than the three items above.

Layering

Layering is a good way to prepare for weather that can suddenly turn warm or cool. For example, a lightweight skirt or pair of pants can be worn with a shirt or blouse in warm weather or with a coordinated wool sweater, jacket or raincoat for cooler weather.

Since jackets and raincoats are bulky, you can wear one or carry it in transit.

Toiletries

Packing all the little, miscellaneous items such as toothbrush and aspirin can often take longer than packing clothes. If you travel frequently or even once a year, you can save time by keeping a leak-proof bag packed with a razor, blades, creams, toothbrush, toothpaste, medicines, hairbrush, comb and other necessities at all times. Then you don't have to gather up all these items every time you pack. All you have to do is grab the bag and place it in your suitcase. Of course, when you return from your trip, be sure to replace the items that are almost gone or worn out.

Travel Gear

Items you always take along on trips—travel alarm clock, tissue packs, extra pair of nylons, plastic rain hat, set of house keys—can be kept together in the same box or bag in a cupboard or drawer. Then you won't have to remember each item separately. Just open your drawer and pack the travel box in your suitcase. To save on space, you can even keep the box in your luggage when you're not traveling.

Electrical Appliances

Electrical appliances can take up much of your suitcase space, especially if you need transformers and special plugs for foreign currents. If you pack clothes that tend not to wrinkle, you won't need an iron, and if you absolutely must take a hair dryer, try to pack it inside something that already takes up space. You could, for example, pack a mini hair dryer (the kind made for traveling) inside a shoe.

Growing Room

If you plan to shop on your trip, don't pack your suitcase full. Leave room to add new purchases, souvenirs and gifts. Another alternative is to pack a smaller, soft tote bag inside the suitcase. Then, when you need it, you can open the tote bag and add the purchases.

Finding a Physician in a Foreign Country*

Following are tips for finding a physician when traveling abroad:

1. Contact the American Embassy or Consulate to request referrals to English-speaking physicians.

2. University teaching hospitals overseas often have English-speaking staff and may be relied upon for good-quality medical care.

3. Prior to departure, travelers can join the International Association for Medical Assistance to Travelers (IAMAT). Services include lists of English-speaking physicians overseas, information on malaria and other tropical diseases and world climate charts.

   > IAMAT
   >
   > 417 Center Street
   >
   > Lewiston, New York 14092-3633
   >
   > (716) 754-4883

4. Individual organizations provide specific travel information and assistance to patients with the following medical conditions: kidney disease, emphysema, diabetes, physical handicaps.

*Compiled by Dr. Claire Panosian, Travel and Tropical Medicine Clinic, University of California at Los Angeles

Travel Checklist

If you keep a checklist in your travel file, along with your tickets and travel notes, you'll know exactly what arrangements you've made and those you still need to take care of before you leave. You can make several copies and attach one inside the front or back cover of the file you keep on each trip. Don't use the original—you'll need it to make more copies. Then just check the items off by writing in the date you finish taking care of each arrangement.

Airline reservations _____ Tickets due _____

Train reservations _____ Tickets _____

Hotel reservations_____

Car rentals _____

Passports _____ Visas_____

Shots_____

Credit card payments _____Rent payment _____

Other payments to be advanced _____

Babysitter _____ Dog sitter or kennel _____

Itinerary left for family and office_____

Copy of will/insurance policies left with family _____

Car checked _____

    Battery fluid _____   Transmission fluid _____

    Coolant _____   Oil _____

First aid kit _____   Tires _____

Spare tire _____   Ski rack _____

Chains _____   Baby seat _____

Tune up _____   Flares _____

Flashlight _____   Car tools _____

Window wipers _____

Home:

Plants watered _____   Mail picked up_____

Housekeeper notified _____   Security patrol notified _____

Newspapers stopped _____   House sitter hired _____

Special Airline Meals

If you have specific dietary needs, you can request special meals on airline flights. The special meals offered will vary according to the airline, the duration of the flight and the time of day. For example, between Los Angeles and New York, you can order a seafood platter on many lunch or dinner flights but not on breakfast flights.

Below are some of the special meals commonly offered on domestic flights designated as meal flights. If you plan to order a special meal, be sure to do so more than 24 hours in advance. There is no extra charge.

Bland	Low calorie
Baby food	Low carbohydrate
Child	Low cholesterol
Diabetic	Low sodium
Fruit plate	Moslem
Infant	Seafood platter
Hindu	Vegetarian
Kosher	Vegetarian, no dairy

Traveler's Health History*

International travelers should carry with them the following information:

1. A current immunization record (preferably, the yellow International Certificates of Vaccination)

2. A list of current medications, including trade name, generic name and dosage

3. A list of medical conditions, such as hypertension, diabetes, cardiac disease (cardiac patients should also bring a copy of a recent electrocardiogram tracing)

4. A list of known drug allergies

5. Eyeglass lens prescription

6. Name and telephone number of regular physician

7. Name and telephone number of relative or friend in the United States to assist in the event of illness overseas

8. Name, telephone number and policy number of medical insurance company

9. If traveling abroad, the telephone number for emergency evacuation service and State Department emergency assistance

*Compiled by Dr. Claire Panosian, Travel and Tropical Medicine Clinic, University of California at Los Angeles

Traveler's Medical Kit*

Prescription drugs (consult physician to determine need)

- Malaria prophylaxis (mefloquine, doxycycline—depending on itinerary)
- Anti-diarrheal medications
- Anti-emetic suppository
- Motion sickness drug
- Sleeping pill or melatonin (to combat jet lag)

Nonprescription drugs

- Aspirin, ibuprofen or acetaminophen
- Antihistamine/decongestant (cold remedy)
- Pepto-Bismol
- Pedialyte (glucose-electrolyte mix for dehydration)
- Water purification tablets or liquid additive

Topical preparations

- Antibiotic ointment
- Insect repellent (containing 20-35 percent DEET and insecticide or permethrin spray)
- Sunscreen
- 0.5 percent cortisone cream
- Iodine solution (wound disinfectant)

Supplies

- Oral thermometer
- Scissors, sterile razor
- Bandages, gauze, tape
- Safety pins

*Compiled by Dr. Claire Panosian, Travel and Tropical Medicine Clinic, University of California at Los Angeles

Your Travel Agent

What to Expect from Your Travel Agent

Your travel agent can assist you in selecting the right destination as well as the right tour, cruise or independent travel arrangements. Travel agents can provide reservations and tickets for airlines, trains, accommodations, and car and limousine rentals and supply useful information on worldwide destinations.

Some travelers hesitate to use a travel agency because of the misconception that prices obtained directly from the airlines and hotels are lower. Otherwise, how could a travel agency make money?

Travel agencies are paid commissions by airlines, hotels, tour operators, cruise lines, car rental agencies, limousine companies and other vendors for the services they sell that are used. Ticket prices are generally the same as those that can be obtained directly from the airline or tour operator, and in some cases, when special contracts are in place, these prices can be lower.

In 1995 the major U.S. airlines placed a cap on the commissions they pay to travel agencies. Previously, agencies were paid 10 percent of the pretax ticket price. Now, with some exceptions, agencies earn 8 percent of the pretax domestic ticket price up to a maximum of $25 for a one-way or $50 for a round trip ticket.

In the past, agencies made up for losses incurred in issuing low-priced tickets with commissions from higher priced tickets. With the caps, however, most agencies have been forced to charge some fees, usually between $10 and $35 for certain transactions, usually for processing refunds, exchanges or low-cost tickets. Then what difference does it make whether you use a travel agent or book your trip yourself?

There are several advantages to using a travel agent even if your arrangements consist solely of an airline ticket to visit family. The major advantage is access and ease of booking. Most travel agencies are automated with one of the major airline systems. Although the airlines are automated, their reservationists will naturally try to sell their product first. So if you call ABC airline, their reservationists will advise you of their flights and only if they can't match you to one of their own flights will they usually advise you of alternatives. If XYZ Airline has a cheaper flight at the same time, chances are you won't hear about it unless you call XYZ Airline directly. If you want the complete picture of all the fares and availabilities between New York and Los Angeles, you could spend a lot of time "surfing the net" or calling the ten or more airlines that serve those two points.

You can do all that work yourself or access those availabilities with one telephone call to a travel agent, where you have the advantage of one-stop shopping.

Since travel agencies have no control over the commission rate set by airlines and other vendors, they can also lose money on some transactions. If you return a refundable ticket unused, the agency must return the commission to the airline. When you add up the cost of staff time, computers, paper forms, tickets, telephone calls and delivery, the agency has lost money on your transaction. And when an airline drops the fare after you have been ticketed to Chicago and you exchange your ticket for the new, lower price, the agent must rewrite the ticket, returning part of the commission to the airline.

Don't confuse fees charged by agencies with cancellation penalties imposed by airlines, tour operators and hotels. If, for example, you cancel a cruise and lose your deposit of $500, it's lost to the cruise company and your agent gets nothing for his or her work unless the agency charges its own cancellation fee as well.

Another reason to use a travel agent is for documentation of transactions. If you arrive at an airline check-in counter only to be told, "Sorry, we don't have your reservation," chances are you won't have any proof of the transaction.

"But I called yesterday and spoke to a Ms. Acron or Aran or Occron or something like that," you say.

"Sorry, we don't show the reservation and this flight is full."

On rare occasions, some computer transactions never get through to the designated airline and instead fall into computer limbo. In most cases, however, a passenger record will show seat assignments or schedule changes that prove the airline received the record.

If your travel agent made this reservation via computer and you advise him or her immediately of the problem, the agent can retrieve the history on your booking record, or PNR (passenger name record), and armed with proof of the transaction, help get you on the flight. Likewise, because travel agents move hundreds of passengers, your travel agent often has more clout when it comes to helping you resolve travel problems.

Travel agencies often provide additional services for free: advance seat assignments; boarding passes; ticket delivery; placement of frequent-flyer numbers in the automated record; itinerary planning; information on passport, visa and inoculation requirements; and general information and brochures on destinations. The trend, however, is to charge for some or all of these services, particularly when travelers are using free tickets or for customized travel itineraries that require many hours of discussion, research, phoning, faxing and typing.

Finally, since most travel agents are in the business because they love to travel, you have not only their own travel experience at your disposal but also the feedback they receive from hundreds of clients like you.

In addition, expect that your travel agent will do the following:

1. Respond to your requests for airline reservations, hotels, car rentals, tours or cruises in a timely fashion or explain the reason for delays.

2. Explain what payments are due and when, along with what fees or penalties may result from the booking, or direct you to the page in the brochure where penalties are specified.

3. Tell you in advance if there will be service charges resulting from long-distance phone calls, faxes, individualized itineraries, refunds, etc.

4. Process refunds, if refunds are due. Keep in mind, however, that in cases where monies have already been sent to other vendors, the agent must wait for the refund from that vendor. Tour operators, for example, often take eight weeks or more to refund payments to the agency.

What Not to Expect from Your Travel Agent

While travel agents can help you with your travel arrangements, you shouldn't expect them to do the following:

1. Most agencies will not absorb international phone calls and faxes or other out-of-pocket expenses.

2. Most agents don't have time to keep track of your frequent-flyer mileage and prizes or to write to the airlines if you forget to give them your frequent-flyer numbers. Agents have hundreds of clients. Keeping track of mileage credits for customers could turn into a full-time occupation with no compensation.

3. While travel agents can request seat assignments on most flights, they can't guarantee that the specific seats passengers want, e.g., window seat, aisle seat, bulkhead seat, will be available. Not all airlines pre-assign seats and some block the best seats for their highest level frequent flyers or full-fare passengers. The best way to get the seat you want is to request it well in advance of the flight, or if the airline does not pre-assign seats, check in early at the airport.

4. Clients sometimes ask, "What's the view like from the rooms on the fifth floor in the International Hotel in Karachi?" or, "Does the bed at our hotel in Corpus Christi have good springs?" No matter how well traveled an agent may be, keep in mind that it's impossible to see every room in every hotel in every country in the world.

5. Some agents will be reluctant to plan a two-week or longer individualized itinerary for free. It's standard for clients to require two or three hotels and a car rental along with their airline reservations. But the piecing together of numerous hotel bookings; air, train and ferry schedules; short tours; and private guides, etc., requires much research and work. Many agencies will charge for this type of planning or require a non-refundable deposit before they begin.

6. Your agent can arrange transportation to weddings or plan honeymoons but may not feel qualified to plan a wedding ceremony. Of course, clients don't come right out and ask for this service but usually start by saying, "We want to get married in Hawaii." Then, after the agent has reserved the hotel, they ask, "Can the hotel arrange to have flowers in the room?" then music, then a minister and, before the agent realizes it, he or she has assumed the responsibilities of wedding coordinator with no compensation.

7. Travel agents are not compensated for making restaurant reservations at your destination, so if you request this service, don't overdo it.

8. Your agent cannot control the weather, airline delays, mishandled baggage, airline food or service, overbooked airlines or hotels (yes, they do overbook), the decline of the dollar or bankruptcies of airlines, cruise lines or tour operators.

Like most professionals, agents can serve you better once they understand your preferences and expectations and what type of traveler you are. Otherwise, they have no way of knowing if you only fly nonstop or if you're willing to change planes twice to save $50.

Sources of Additional Information

Contact universities and colleges for a catalogue of their study/travel tours. Your local travel agent can direct you to specialty tours and cruises. Contact numbers for tour companies and organizations mentioned in this book are listed below.

AESU
22 Hamill Road, Ste. 248
Baltimore, MD 21210-1807
(800) 638-7640
(410) 323-4416
Fax (410) 323-4498
http://AESU.com

Animal Animal Care USDA,
Aphis, Ac
4700 River Road, Unit 84
Riverdale, MD 20737-1234
(301) 734-7833
http://www.Aphis.USDA.gov/ac

American Field Service
National Service Center
198 Madison Avenue
New York, NY 10016
(212) 299-9000
Fax (212) 299-9090
Information Center
310 SW 4th Ave., Ste. 630
Portland, OR 97204-2608
800-237-4636
Fax (503) 241-1653
http://www.AFS.org

Club Europa
802 W. Oregon St.
Urbana, IL 61801
(800) 777-9344
(217) 344-5863
http://osgweb.com/tour/ClubEuropa

Club Mediterranee
7976 N. Hayden Road
Scottsdale, AZ 85258-5246
(800) 258-2633
Fax (800) 727-5306
http://www.ClubMed.com/

Contiki Holidays
300 Plaza Alicante, #900
Garden Grove, CA 92840
(714) 740-0808
Fax (714) 740-0818
http://www.contiki.com

Earthwatch Headquarters
680 Mount Auburn St.
P.O. Box 9104
Watertown, MA 02272-9104
(800) 776-0188
(617) 926-8200
E-mail: info@earthwatch.org
http://www.earthwatch.org

Elderhostel
75 Federal St.
Boston, MA 01220-1841
(617) 426-7788
http://www.Elderhostel.org

Gritti Palace
Campo San Maria del Giglio
Venice, Italy 30124
Phone (011)(39)(41) 794-611
Fax (011)(39)(41) 520-0924
Or contact Sheraton Hotels
Luxury Collection 800-325-3535
http://www.ITTSheraton.com

IAMAT (International Association
for Medical Assistance to
Travellers)
417 Center St.
Lewiston, NY 14092-3633
(716) 754-4883
http://www.sentex.net/iamat

Specialty Travel Index
305 San Anselmo Avenue
San Anselmo, CA 94960
(415) 459-4900
Fax (415) 459-4974
http://www.Spectrav.com

Index

Order Form

Telephone orders: (888) 837-2665

On-line orders: http://www.upperaccess.com/catalog.htm

Fax/mail orders: Photocopy this form and fax it to (800) 242-0036 or mail to Upper Access Books, P.O. Box 457, Hinesburg, VT 05451.

Please send _____ copies of *How to Travel with Others without Wishing They'd Stayed Home* at $16.95 each plus $3.00 shipping. If you are a resident of Vermont, add $0.70 sales tax to each copy. Shipping time: USA 1–2 weeks; Outside USA: 2–3 weeks.

I understand that I may return any books in resalable condition for a full refund within 45 days of purchase.

Name: _____

Address: _____

_____

_____

Telephone: _____ Fax: _____ E-mail _____

Form of payment:

❏ Check or money order enclosed - total $ _____

❏ Visa ❏ MasterCard ❏ Amex ❏ Discover - total $ _____

Card number: _____Exp date: _____

Print name on card: _____

Signature: _____

For all other inquiries, contact Prince Publishing, 11718 Barrington Ct. 514, Los Angeles, CA 90049 USA, Phone: (310) 472-0548, Fax: (310) 471-4677, E-mail: PrincePub@aol.com.